A FALL OF 𝒲oodcock

A Season's Worth of Tales on Hunting
a Most Elusive Little Game Bird

Tom Huggler

*Introduction
by Charley Waterman*

*Illustrations
by Jim Foote*

Skyhorse Publishing

Copyright © 1996 by Tom Huggler
Illustrations © 1996 by Jim Foote

First Skyhorse Publishing edition 2014
Introduction © 2014 by Charley F. Waterman

All rights reserved. No part of this book may be reproduced in any manner without the express written consent of the publisher, except in the case of brief excerpts in critical reviews or articles. All inquiries should be addressed to Skyhorse Publishing, 307 West 36th Street, 11th Floor, New York, NY 10018.

Skyhorse Publishing books may be purchased in bulk at special discounts for sales promotion, corporate gifts, fund-raising, or educational purposes. Special editions can also be created to specifications. For details, contact the Special Sales Department, Skyhorse Publishing, 307 West 36th Street, 11th Floor, New York, NY 10018 info@skyhorsepublishing.com.

Skyhorse® and Skyhorse Publishing® are registered trademarks of Skyhorse Publishing, Inc.®, a Delaware corporation.

Visit our website at www.skyhorsepublishing.com.

10 9 8 7 6 5 4 3 2 1

Library of Congress Cataloging-in-Publication Data is available on file.

Cover painting by Jim Foote
Illustrations by Jim Foote

Print ISBN: 978-1-62914-602-7
Ebook ISBN: 978-1-62914-944-8

Printed in the United States of America

For Ellen VanDeMark
for showing the way

COLOR PLATES

Plate I   *Double Flush and Setter*

Plate II   *1986 RGS Stamp Print*

Palte III *Tom Huggler and Fagin*

Plate IV   *Brittanies and Woodcock*

Plate V   *Woodcock Pair*

Contents

ACKNOWLEDGMENTS vii
INTRODUCTION by Charley Waterman xii
PROLOGUE 1
  1   FLEDGLINGS 11
  2   PARTNERS 25
  3   NEW ENGLAND 41
  4   THE MARITIMES 65
  5   MAINE 95
  6   A 28-GAUGE TRIBUTE 109
  7   LOUISIANA 123
  8   MICHIGAN 151
  9   BIRD CAMP 181
 10   RESEARCHERS 197
 11   OLD HANDS 217
EPILOGUE 233
ABOUT THE AUTHOR 241
ABOUT THE ARTIST 241

Acknowledgments

Many people helped make this book possible, including a host of friends and acquaintences whose names are contained within. They shared their private woodcock coverts, invited me into their homes, answered my incessant questions, and put up with my muddy dogs and bad jokes.

I wish to thank Art DeLaurier Jr. and Angela Saxon for steering this book through the process of judicious editing, design, layout, and printing. The work is as much theirs as it is mine.

It also belongs to Jim Foote and his wife, Joanne, who encouraged the idea from the outset. They supported it with enthusiasm and graciously contributed all the artwork between these covers.

I owe special thanks to my wife, Laura, who has a better ear for language than I do, especially when the words are my own.

fall: *an alleged name for a covey or flight (of woodcock). Obsolete. Circa 1430.*

Oxford English Dictionary

To travel well within your neighborhood is the greatest of journeys.

> Samuel Johnson

Introduction

by Charley F. Waterman

Woodcock hunting tends to be for life, as it seems to be for Tom Huggler. The little game bird with the great mysteries has long attracted fine writing from fine writers, but few author-gunners have followed it as Huggler has. His travels are similar to those of the bird itself, guided by season, weather, and even rumor.

His book is filled with woodcock knowledge but runs almost as a gunner's autobiography, beginning with juvenile operations and typical youthful armament and going through the serious hunter's trial-and-error choices until he has drawn his own personal conclusions about things like guns and loads. But he does not let the practical sides of woodcock shooting or woodcock biology interfere with the important part—the sentiment that clings forever to the woodcock follower, his dogs of today and yesteryear, and the autumn winds and weather that guide the fragile subjects to ordained destinations.

Tom Huggler tells of woodcock hunters, guides, and researchers from Canada's Maritimes to Louisiana and he lives very near to both woodcock and woodcock watchers in

INTRODUCTION

Michigan. His travels have frequently been in motor homes and his routes are obviously changed with news from the skimpy woodcock grapevines.

Like others who live much of the time in travel rigs with dogs and guns, Tom Huggler is likely to go into considerable detail concerning food and wine and reveals some opinions on woodcock recipes, while giving the impression of being pleased that less fortunate outdoorsmen consider woodcock unfit for consumption.

The Huggler bird dogs have varied from family treasures to hopeless bums, but we feel that some of the bums have, nevertheless, been valued companions. He wryly tells of his misjudgments on woodcock dogs and confides that he now feels any gun dog should make a start with a professional trainer. Some of this is uncomfortably close to home for upland gunners who recognize their own fumbles in the writer's canine misfires, but a bird shooting reader is likely to feel he is dealing comfortably with a kindred soul, which he is. This is a woodcock authority who has paid his dues, and the reader squirms with him when the gun somehow doesn't track and is relieved when Huggler begins to hit again with a new shotgun or a new approach.

Good teachers are likely to be good students and this writer gains woodcock knowledge as he goes and looks forward to tomorrow's revelations. He treats known woodcock experts with respect, and even reverence, and has a special regard for the veterans of today and yesteryear who have traced the little ghost birds through their times of plenty and adversity. Woodcock are important to him and his readers feel it.

Although he has followed woodcock for all those years he leaves the impression that each day with his beloved aspens or abandoned railway grades is likely to reveal some treasure of new information about them. He complains mildly about

A Fall of Woodcock

the hunting restrictions that come with advancing age and apprehensively wonders about his next twenty or thirty years. There is the feeling that his views are those of all the world's woodcock hunters.

Here with the carefully researched facts and figures from well-known woodcock authorities, including biologists (he seems to know most of such people), are his own observations about wind and weather that seem pleasingly out of place with the relaxed narrative of a wandering gunner. It appears, he says, that woodcock follow highways as well as rivers—but are they sure of the difference as they ride the chill of autumn night winds?

There is a ridiculous feeling that woodcock may have helped write this book.

—Charley F. Waterman

Prologue

A friend and I were driving through Ontario's Algonquin Park one May morning when he suddenly slammed on the brakes, his van squealing to a halt. "Sorry," he apologized, "but I didn't want to hit that bird."

"Bird?" I wondered, recomposing myself and thankful that he didn't put me through the windshield because I wasn't wearing a seat belt.

My friend pointed to the asphalt, and sure enough a buff-colored bird with a lance for a bill wobbled across the highway like a bowling pin about to tip over.

"It's a woodcock," I said and jumped out for a better look. A yard or so behind the hen bird in single file marched four yellow-and-brown chicks that looked like overgrown bumblebees with gigantic, misplaced stingers. That was the first and only time I have ever stopped traffic to assist a family of woodcock across a road.

Woodcock have fascinated me most of my life. Although the incident occurred many years ago, I remember it well. A mile farther down the road, my friend braked his van once again to avoid hitting a moose. This time I was wearing my seat belt.

It is the woodcock encounter that I remember with greater clarity, and so it is often that way with the smaller wild things. No sailfish or huge Chinook salmon adorn my office walls. In their place are a three-pound brook trout and a twenty-one-inch-long grayling. Upstairs in the living room, no deer and bear heads stare into space with glass eyes, but native grouse and quail peer out from glass-encased dioramas.

I have no aversion to big game. I hunt elk and caribou and deer and am happy that the morning's mail brought an antlerless whitetail permit. It is just that I love small game more. I enjoy teasing a hand-sized bluegill into hitting a popper so tiny I can barely thread the line through it with these myopic eyes of mine. I like to stalk little streams for brook trout with a fly rod, and I like to hunt birds. The diminutive ones—Hungarian partridge, quail, woodcock—I especially prize.

Prologue

A few years ago several friends and I booked a hunt for speckle-bellied geese with an outfitter along the Gulf Coast of Louisiana. It was mid-January and the hard-hunted birds were call-shy and spread-shy. Averaging only one goose each during the first couple days of hunting, we were thinking of cutting short the hunt. But I had been noticing large numbers of snipe probing for food in nearby drained rice fields and crayfish ponds. Over supper I suggested to our guides that we organize a drive.

"You nuts?" one of them said. "You could never hit them little dicky birds. There ain't but two bites of meat on 'em anyway."

Imagine eleven drab men wearing hip boots and waders, in a long curving line like a scimitar, marching across mud flats, retrievers at heel wondering what this foolishness is all about. Picture the men turned into happy, hollering boys again as they empty their guns at the batlike snipe that jink away in all directions. We shot nearly a case of shells—five hundred rounds—that day and killed only thirty-eight birds. Thirty-nine, actually, because one of my friends found a dead snipe in his coveralls pocket the next morning. We delivered the birds to a Lafayette restaurant where the chef prepared a Cajun snipe gumbo so delicious I believe I can still taste it.

The snipe, of course, is a shore bird. His slightly larger cousin, *Scolopax minor*, evolved from marshlands to uplands to the absolute delight of those of us who seek him. The American woodcock is one of the continent's few upland game birds that is migratory (the others are doves), and the only one that we hunt with pointing dogs. This oddity gives woodcock a singular mysteriousness and makes them highly unpredictable. Woodcock hunting always involves hunches because who can say with certainty where the bird is today or where it is going tonight? It is simple sport, unencumbered by mechanization unless you count a dog bell, compass, and an improved-cylinder choke tube sophisticated gadgetry.

I don't. To me, the woodcock is our finest game bird, and I live to hunt him each fall. It is always too long between Octobers.

Summers are the hardest. In Michigan our sixty-day-long hunting season ends November 14. Walking to deer-hunting stands and back to the car again, I have jumped late migrants through November, and other hunters I know have flushed woodcock even into December. If you miss woodcock when northern coverts grow bare of leaves and birds, you can migrate south and hunt them after the new year, as I have. You can see woodcock come back in March, and you can hunt them in April and May and even in June with your friends, the certified banders. But summer is long. Too long. I realize that on a July morning when I sort through a stack of color slides, choosing images to illustrate a magazine article.

There's Larry, an old Iowa buddy who began trading me pheasant hunts for woodcock forays years ago. Is it three years now, or four, since I shared that

PROLOGUE

bird-full covert? And there is Macbeth in a classic point. She didn't always cock a foreleg like that. Didn't usually stick her haughty setter head *that* high to suck up bird scent. Next is a scene right out of a Jim Foote painting: Black water of the tiny pond freighting orange maple leaves. The green bracken fern bleeding to yellow and brown under the gaunt birches. The Brittanies on point. The woodcock frozen in time. Through the ten-power loupe I swear I can smell the new richness of decaying woods in the celluloid itself.

A Fall of Woodcock

On an August evening we sit at one of those curbside Paris cafes near Hotel de Ville, my new bride and I and another American couple—who, coincidentally, are celebrating their fifth anniversary—sipping a *digestif* and talking about how the city is relatively deserted in August (the month the French go on vacation) and other subjects of insignificance. Dusk is gathering and with it come pools of light beneath the street lamps and a decided coolness to the slight breeze. A jaundiced leaf, curled dead perhaps from pollution, skips across our white linen tablecloth. Grabbing the leaf, I open it and hold it to the light. Round and slightly serrated, the leaf looks like that of an aspen. "What does this remind you of?" I ask my friend Tom.

"Grouse and woodcock hunting," Tom says without hesitation. "What does it make you think of?"

"That and Bird Camp," I reply. "In six weeks we'll be there, again."

Tom smiles. Our wives share knowing glances and resume their conversation.

The French have long revered the European woodcock (*Scolopax rusticola*), learning, over centuries, creative ways to prepare the bird for table and naming fine wines after it. French painters prized the woodcock's primary wingfeathers (*la plume du peintre*) for their fineness and delicacy. Recently a Montreal friend sent me a small bottle of Belgian

PROLOGUE

beer called *Gueuze de la Becasse*, which I drank after shooting my first woodcock of the new hunting season.

"The French kill as many woodcock (2 million annually) as are killed in the entire United States," writes Guy de la Valdene in *Making Game: An Essay on Woodcock* (Clark City Press, 1985), a wonderful book that every bird hunter should have in the home library. The author weaves personal experience with deep research on how woodcock evolved, their life histories, and other unusual facts. The information is as eye-opening as William Sheldon's *The Book of the American Woodcock* (University of Massachusetts Press, 1967) was nearly twenty years earlier.

If you want tactical information on how to hunt woodcock successfully, I suggest, among others, John Alden Knight's classic *Woodcock* (Alfred A. Knopf, 1944, reprinted by Gunnerman Press, 1989), Frank Woolner's *Timberdoodle* (Crown Publishers, Inc., 1974), Steve Smith's *Woodcock Shooting* (Stackpole Books, 1988) or Don L. Johnson's *Grouse & Woodcock: A Gunner's Guide* (Krause Publications, 1995). A fine anthology of essays on the joys of woodcock hunting is *Come October* (Countrysport Press, 1991). More good reading can be found in *Timberdoodle Tales* by Tom F. Waters (Riparian Press, 1993).

This book is different. It is a personal journey through landscapes both exterior and interior. In spite of dozens of research projects and nearly forty years of banding records, precious little is known about woodcock. We know even less about ourselves. Maybe my journey will become your journey, too, as we travel together with that other wanderlust, the American woodcock.

                                      Tom Huggler
                                      Sunfield, Michigan

1

FLEDGLINGS

Do you remember the first woodcock you ever shot? I can recall the first ring-necked pheasant, the first ruffed grouse, the first snowshoe hare that made its satisfying way into the game bag of my too-large hunting coat, a hand-me-down from my father. Try as I might, though, I can't recapture that first woodcock.

But I do remember the first woodcock I ever *saw*. The incident occurred in the late 1950s when I was about fourteen years old. Several of us boys were hunting pheasants with our fathers and older brothers in southern Michigan when a few of our party split up and entered a stand of frost-tinged hardwoods, largely maples. Suddenly, a small brown bird with oversized wings jumped up and danced away as though on puppet strings.

"What the hell was that?" someone hollered.

"Woodcock!" one of the older boys shouted. Then another bird flushed. "Shoot 'em!"

I was toting a Mossberg 20-gauge bolt action (remember the model with the green- and red-colored thumb safety behind the bolt?). Even though I had bagged my first pheasant and blue-winged teal with that gun, I could not hit one of these new, speedy targets that cut a Zorro-like swath through the trees before topping out and disappearing. Working after school sacking groceries for fifty cents an hour, I was very stingy with the dark-green Remington shells I bought for pheasant hunting. After wasting an afternoon's labor on woodcock that pogo-sticked above the undergrowth then whisked away to safety, I decided to save my hard-earned ammo.

"They ain't no good to eat anyway," one of the older boys said. "They eat worms. I don't even shoot at 'em anymore."

As pheasant numbers declined—a phenomenon that began in the early sixties in the Midwest—we began hunting partridge, or "pats," with increased enthusiasm. Woodcock often contributed to our mixed bags. While still in high school, I began to hunt both birds with keen interest in the vicinity of Sand Lake in eastcentral lower Michigan, where David Pringle, a cousin of my girlfriend, spent weekends and often asked me to tag along. David's grandmother,

Fledglings

who came to Michigan in a covered wagon from the East, lived alone in an old house on the shores of Sand Lake. She sent us afield "full as ticks" after an enormous breakfast of pancakes and sausage, which we tamped down with black coffee. We killed grouse on the same state lands we hunted deer. We shot woodcock along streams we fished earlier in the year for brook trout.

To this day, there is no form of bird hunting I enjoy more than wandering down old railroad rights-of-way while my dog casts through the brush that grows heavy on both sides. Or when I'm in a canoe, impatient dog in the bow, on a lonely river, and stopping here and there to probe the wet tangles of the bottom ground for flight woodcock.

Melvin Trobaugh, an older friend of mine who saved his money to buy a Charles Daly over-under and who learned how to shoot it, once killed sixteen grouse and woodcock without a miss. Like all my friends, at day's end Melvin readily agreed to divide the collective bag among the participants. Woodcock, their once-bright eyes now filmy and sunken, their lion-colored breast feathers no longer soft but matted with dried dog spittle, were always the last to go.

"Take mine," was an offer commonly made. "My ma won't cook 'em anyway."

In those days no one hunted woodcock purely on the bird's own merits. They were either ignored or taken incidentally while seeking other game. With one exception. As a kid, I heard stories of men who "dusked" woodcock—that is, illegally shot them just before dark when the birds flew from daytime haunts and were silhouetted against the light of late day. One afternoon while hunting around a gypsum quarry near National City in Iosco County, Michigan, I came across evidence of a violent scene that puzzled me. Two wooden orange crates sat empty and upended in an open spot surrounded by brush and piles of overburden. Dozens of shotshell hulls lay around the crates.

Fledglings

This was obviously a killing ground, but for what I had no idea. After sundown I was walking through the pit back to my car when I heard voices. The gunners, two men in their fifties, explained to me how they sat back to back on the orange crates and blasted away at dipping and darting woodcock until their barrels grew warm to the touch. Speaking in animated tones, they said it was a lot of fun.

"You can see flame shoot out the gun barrel!" one of them said.

"What do you do with the birds?" I remember asking.

"Oh, the Lab finds some, but the rest just die out there somewhere. Don't matter. They taste like liver, and I hate liver."

When market hunting was legal, woodcock were slaughtered for profit. In the South on winter nights, hunters carried pine torches to feeding fields where the birds' high-set eyes easily showed. Using sticks, they killed woodcock by the thousands and sold them for pennies each in New Orleans restaurants. Apparently New York City diners prized them more highly—one 1874 account says woodcock sold there for $1.50 per brace.

William Mershon, who lived near Saginaw and chronicled fifty years of hunting and fishing in Michigan during the period 1870 to 1920, wrote about hunting woodcock as early as the Fourth of July. Why? In those days before hunting seasons and bag limits, woodcock were the first young-of-the-year game birds to be flying. Bags of fifty to one hundred woodcock were not uncommon in Michigan, New York State, and New England, although by 1900 the birds were in serious population decline. In 1902 a writer named A. K. Fisher referred to woodcock and wood ducks as "two vanishing game birds." (*Yearbook U.S.D.A.*). E. Sandys and T. S. Van Dyke, writing in 1904 (*Upland Game Birds*, Macmillan), said, "Good cock-shooting is now almost a thing of the past in many places where heavy bags were the rule."

Market hunting, of course, ended with the Migratory Bird Treaty Act of 1918, but the desire for big, illegal kills will always take root in the heart of the renegade. A few years ago a man I contacted through a friend invited me to his Deep South duck-hunting camp in December. "Come on down," he said into the phone. You can kill a hundred woodcock in two hours if you want to. I have absolutely no respect for the damn things." I didn't go. Recently, I learned the man was arrested by federal agents for game-law violations.

It took me a long time to learn that you cannot introduce women to bird hunting and always expect them to embrace the sport with the same enthusiasm that you do. I have spent a small fortune on guns, boots, and specialty clothing in a lifelong attempt to find partners to share this form of love with me. The most passionate ones—and I have hunted with several—were already spoken for. When I was younger, I determined the cut-off age for a woman's initial exposure to the blood sports—with the great hope that the experience would take root and grow—was about twenty-five years.

Now I'm not so sure.

I recently agreed to guide two women on their first-ever grouse and woodcock hunt. Both are proficient in the use of firearms. One, in her early forties, is an NRA-certified shooting instructor who leads seminars called "Purse/Sonal Protection," which includes Lady's Elite Firearm Training. The other, twenty-seven and also a married mother, is a writer who covers hunting, fishing, and camping; she is also a much sought-after teacher in the increasingly popular Becoming an Outdoors Woman program. The women were great sports—full of curiosity and optimism—in spite of the rainy day and the fact they bagged none of the nineteen woodcock we flushed.

One of the reasons I hunt birds with such zeal is that I never feel more alive than when I'm hoofing it up some mountain or wading through a sea of bluestem or aspen or cattails following a dog in search of a bird. Any bird. A Trappist monk in his late seventies once told a friend of mine that hunting and fishing pursuits have a deep spiritual side to them, a personal quest or seeking that most people do not admit to. Some, perhaps most of us, seek to turn defiance into a personal understanding of who we are and why we do what we do. When we understand, maybe we can accept. If we can accept, perhaps we can connect with others. Are we here for some other purpose?

Every hunt, but especially those with woodcock in the plan, is delightful, even if it rains and there are no birds. Of course, you remember best those days of golden October light, of starch-stiff points, of coverts groaning with birds. About fifteen years ago, I traded in my high-school teacher's book of lesson plans for one containing editorial calendars. During that first autumn of being gainfully underemployed as a full-time freelance writer, I tried to do many of the things I had wanted to do but couldn't because of the classroom. I shot a whitetail with a bow and then a prime black bear. One of my goals was to intercept flight woodcock at the exact time they descended on Michigan's Drummond Island.

At 250 square miles this hunter's paradise lies at the bottom of the Saint Marys River, where it sweeps into northern Lake Huron at the eastern end of the Upper Peninsula. Access from the mainland is via car ferry. After what seemed an eternity, weather conditions turned prime. A cold front was moving across Canada, forcing birds south with favorable northwest winds. Sandi, my wife at that time, did not hunt but wanted to go north to see the fall colors, so we hitched a small trailer to my pickup truck, loaded our young setter, Lady Macbeth, and headed out the morning of the big freeze.

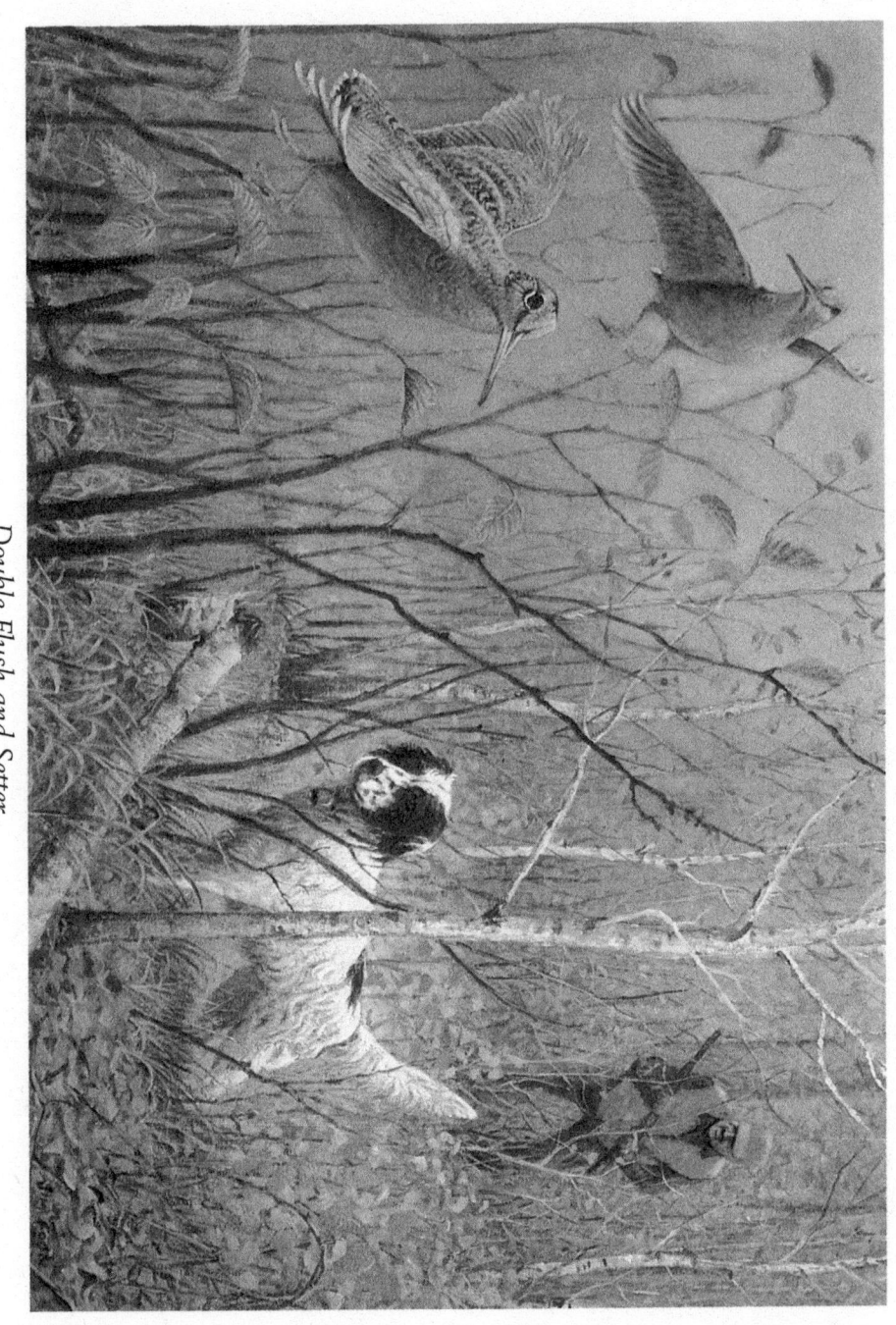

Double Flush and Setter
by Jim Foote

Plate I

Fledglings

Driving past the school where I used to teach, I confess to a pang of remorse, but the open road lay ahead and three hundred miles later we plunged deep into October with its "hectic" reds—as the poet Shelley said—and vibrant yellows. The school fell farther and farther into my rear-view mirror. Noun clauses were a thing of the past. Shakespeare lectures a light-year away. There was no turning back now, and it felt good to be alive, though I hadn't a clue where the next paycheck was coming from.

Arriving at the campground in late afternoon, I disengaged and leveled the trailer, turned on the lights, kissed my wife goodbye, and drove down old trails looking for woodcock habitat. Finding a promising covert, I unloaded Macbeth, then realized I had left my gun in the trailer. We went hunting anyway and we found woodcock in the lowlands,

which had yet to freeze. The birds, tired from their long flight, rested under junipers and in dry islands of dogwood and witch hazel. Every few yards, it seemed, Macbeth would go on point, foreleg cocked, eyes watering, tail straight as a pool cue. Once more, I was falling in love with a young dog.

After the fifth or sixth flush I could stand it no longer. Racing back to the trailer, I burst in the door. Without a word my wife handed me the gun, then went back to reading a mystery she had brought along. "Supper will be ready when you get back," she said, smiling.

I killed five woodcock with five shells while the sun hung expectantly like the New Year's Eve ball poised in Times Square. We went on, farther into the covert, and Macbeth stuck and held another dozen birds, which I goosed aloft, until the owls began calling. Woodsmoke hung over the campground when we returned, and I could smell bear steaks sizzling through the screen door of our little trailer. Shoving a drink in my hand, my wife wondered if I had a bit of an appetite. That night I lost myself with her all over again, and with my dog and woodcock, even though they left in the night and Sandi dropped out of my life a couple of years later. Macbeth lived to the ripe old age of eight.

Closer to home and a little deeper into that fall, Macbeth and I stumbled upon a drop of woodcock in a covert that framed an old pasture. We gunned our way down one side and back up the other during seventh-hour literature class. I thought I heard the ringing bell that signified class change, but it was only the tinkling of my dog's bell. Happy, expansively carefree, on the way home I stopped in a neighboring town and bought a thousand-dollar oak dinette set that Sandi had had her eye on. She took it with her, but I kept the slim double barrel I had bought for her, which she never fired, during our crazy courtship.

Woodcock hunting can be an intensely private affair. What you bring to upland coverts and what you take from them is as personal as religious choice, political orientation, or sexual proclivity. I often think better and understand things more clearly after I have hunted alone. And yet I have never spent a memorable day alone in the woods without thinking about old friends, some gone and some still living, and wishing they were along to share my joy.

On an October afternoon of 1983, I talked my aging father into joining me on a woodcock hunt at a state game area not far from home. Although Dad had introduced me to bird hunting, he was no expert bird hunter himself. In spite of owning an occasional good one, his dogs were never trained. He didn't shoot skeet or trap to keep his eye sharp. He hunted with an old Winchester Model 12 pump. Full choke. And he used No. 6 shot for just about everything, including woodcock.

A Fall of Woodcock

I had a good setter and Lab that fall and both performed to perfection the afternoon Dad and I hunted together. I shot a limit of five woodcock with my 20-gauge Citori tubed skeet and improved-cylinder. Then I gave the gun and a pocketful of 8s to my birdless father, who couldn't hit anything with his Model 12. I have a photo of him walking fast along a dirt road with those patented ground-gobbling strides of his, my Lab at heel, a pair of woodcock in his hand. The aspens blazing with yellow fire all around him. "Helluva hunt," I remember him saying.

We got out together one other time. A couple of weeks later found us in a pontoon boat turned duck blind with a friend of mine and his retired father. A big wind tore across Lake Huron, which detoured strings of ducks into the calm safety of Harbor Beach. That wild afternoon we shot twenty-some ducks, mostly scaup and bufflehead, along with a few mergansers and a couple of goldeneyes. Our fathers liked each other, and they took turns taking the easy shots over the decoys. "Best duck hunt I ever had," Dad told me on the drive home. "Thanks."

He died of stomach cancer the next June. During the illness I was able to thank him and to tell him goodbye, something many sons do not get to do. But three months would pass before I could fully acknowledge the loss. It happened in interior Alaska, where a friend and I spent six weeks hunting and fishing that summer and fall. One September afternoon we were rolling down the Denali Highway when I demanded that Ron, my partner, stop the Jeep, fast. A hundred yards off the road, a grove of aspen fluttered pure gold against an infinite sky of Pacific blue. Jumping out, I raced for the trees, the pressure in my throat as painful as though someone had planted a fist there.

In my grief I could see my father coming out of those woods, the little gun over his shoulder, a brace of woodcock in his hand.

Partners

When someone asked me recently how many dogs I've hunted behind, I confessed I did not know. Nor am I sure how many dogs have owned me over more than forty years of chasing game.

Our mother says my two brothers and I went through thirty-eight four-legged partners during an active changing of the guard in our backyard kennel. When I left home at nineteen, I took along a couple of golden retrievers. No one missed them. Over the years, many Labs and goldens have shared duck-blind sandwiches with me. Many more setters, the odd beagle, and an occasional Brittany and shorthair have invited themselves to my tailgate parties in the woods and prairies, fields and foothills of North America.

A Fall of Woodcock

Some dogs were good; two or three bordered on being great. Others were scoundrels that ran deer or hunted for themselves. Some, I swear, could not hear, and a few behaved so shabbily I'm embarrassed to impart details. Unfortunately, the worst ones always knew enough to come home for supper. Many are a memory blur because they were, at best, only average. I'm sure most of them measured me with the same set of scales.

One of the least likely to succeed was a mongrel puppy we called Prince, who came into our lives when I was about ten. Prince taught my brothers, our friends, and me how to hunt pheasants in southern Michigan during the last great wave of ringnecks in the mid-1950s. We'll never see those days again. And I will never have another dog like Prince again.

At the time, my older brother was a teenager selling subscriptions door-to-door for *Life* and other magazines. He plucked the collie–springer spaniel mix from an under-the-porch litter of a woman who was not interested in buying anything. "But wouldn't you like to take home a puppy?" she begged. "Please."

Prince bonded to us boys the way airplane glue stuck to balsa. He helped us watch our fishing bobbers—barking when they jiggled from a bite—and he guarded our tent flap with the stoic vigilance of a Roman centurion. There was nothing remarkable about Prince's appearance: nondescript coat of clay, mud-colored eyes, stubby legs. His pointy ears and anteater's snout were a gift from his collie father. Prince reminded me of a thirty-pound armadillo with fur.

His hunting prowess was purely instinctual because he received no training. In truth, he became the teacher, a trait I've since discovered that all great dogs exhibit. Prince quickly figured out how ringnecks liked to skulk, double-back, and hunker down into the barest of cover, all the better to hide their Technicolor coats. This bright little dog nearly always led us boys to birds, but we were too ignorant to realize what a prize we owned.

I have since walked beside a few springers at disobedient heel, and once they catch a snootful of pheasant scent, the race is on. But Prince never hunted beyond range of our 20-gauge shotguns. He cast as perfectly as a new pair of windshield wipers. He always checked back, and he watched for our hand signals. He was a wonderful hunting partner and friend.

I can see him now, bounding through the weed stubble on those short coilspring legs, looking back with a happy grin. If Prince had a fault, it was his nonchalance as a retriever (especially when it came to picking up woodcock), and yet we were equally at fault because we often beat him to the fallen birds.

Pride was another weakness, but who can blame a dog, any dog, for showing dignity? In January of my senior year of high school, a physics teacher whose class I was failing offered to give me a sensitive (in other words, "gun-shy") beagle he no longer wanted. Hoping for better grades, I took in the frightened, nervous dog and kept her in the garage. Her name was Peggy.

Prince refused to enter and took to pacing outside until he wore a path in the snow. Looking back some thirty-five years now, I'm sure the distraught Prince was trying to make up his mind what to do about Peggy, the new threat. Two days later he ran away from home, and we never saw him again.

For the longest time, whenever I spotted a neighborhood mongrel with a sharp face, dwarfish legs, and a coat the color of bank-run gravel, I wondered if Prince could be the father. I still remember him well and think about him often.

"I'm convinced there are three good hunting dogs—English setters, English setters, and English setters." So wrote my close friend, the late Ken Lowe, who edited *Michigan Out-of-Doors* for many years and who was my frequent companion in grouse and woodcock coverts. Like Ken, I admit to a huge tender spot for English setters, and I think I know why.

My earliest recollections of bird hunting were behind the family setter, a wide-running rogue named Queenie. I can remember my father hollering and swearing at Queenie as she flushed southern Michigan pheasants from fields a considerable distance from the guns—a speck of white in the middle of all those pretty roosters. It is quite possible that the dog's errant behavior was my fault. After all, I let her run wild each night in the brown sweep of weed fields behind our rural home. I was seven years old and in the second grade. The year was 1952.

I don't remember Queenie finding woodcock, nor do I recall any of the other dogs we owned ever turning up woodcock, or grouse for that matter, although some of them no doubt did. What I do remember is that my father loved to barter. Most of his dogs were poor performers—trade bait for other things like leaky mallard decoys—and none was ever trained.

I, too, have been owned by a legion of pointers, flushers, and retrievers. If the dog has a nose for game and is true to the law of its blood, there is always room at the inn. The mavericks who go their own untrainable way or who lack the desire and ability to be good citizens and solid performers in the field eventually find a No Vacancy sign, although I admit to holding on to certain problem dogs much longer than I should have. I used to subscribe to the assumption that I could turn things around but have learned that most of the time I could not. I am not a professional dog trainer or breeder, although I've managed to fumble both and still put an occasional star in my kennel.

When hunting dogs don't measure up to expectations, all too often we accept the substandard performance. Some of us even make excuses for the underachiever. Surely you've said or have heard said: "He's having a bad day," or "That's odd—she's never done that before," or "Well, at least he found the bird." If you have patience, skill, and time on your hands, you can often correct problems like hard mouth, flagging on point, and refusal to retrieve. Or if you have the money, a professional trainer can straighten out such nuisance behavior, assuming the dog has intelligence and the temperament to learn.

Most do. In fact, proof in many cases that the dog is plenty smart is that he no longer performs as well as he did (setters, for example, often retrieve as puppies, then quit after the first year). Being a clever animal and ever so willing to test his owner, the dog has learned that he can get by with less effort. You, perhaps being a bit lazy yourself or maybe confused by your dog's behavior, accept this new level of mediocrity.

A setter I once owned drove me crazy like that. Chaucer was a handsome tricolored male with a black eye patch. He was one of two eight-month-olds left from a litter I was rearing when I inadvertently brought a parvovirus into the kennel. Earlier in the day I had been playing with a friend's young charge that, unknown to either of us at the time, was ill. The next day I sold the last female, Mardi, from the litter, and the day after that had to rush a prone, near-dead Chaucer to the hospital where for several days whether he would live or die was as tenuous as a flip of the coin.

PARTNERS

The mysterious parvovirus can strike and kill a young dog within hours; fortunately, I had told the new owners, Glen and Martha Eberly of Bloomfield Township, Michigan, to be on the lookout for signs of stress. Even so, they nearly lost Mardi, too. The vet bills and emotional harangue from this incident were enough to make me rethink my role as a dog owner. It is one of the key reasons why I no longer breed dogs today.

Sickly and emaciated, Chaucer lost that first hunting year altogether, but luckily, my year-old female, a setter named Macbeth who was destined for near-greatness, was coming on. Chaucer acted oddly after his illness. He was naturally a bit independent from the start (something I look for in a dog), but his behavior went beyond often-typical male-setter stubbornness. At times Chaucer could be incorrigible—not coming when called, even breaking the occasional point when he felt like it.

Feeling sorry for him, I unwisely made excuses. "Maybe his brain got fried from the high fever," I told a friend after Chaucer bit him when he tried to pry a ring-necked pheasant from the dog's vicelike jaws. "I don't think he can help it," I would always say.

Sure he couldn't. And never mind that the other pup, Mardi, went on to become one of the finest gun-dog setters ever bred for her new owners.

During the summer of Chaucer's second year, I sent him for professional training. "He's no

Macbeth," said Dale Jarvis, the head trainer I've relied upon for years at Hunter's Creek Club in Metamora, Michigan, "but I think that with enough experience he'll be okay. He's tough and he's got a stubborn streak, but he's under control."

Then I did the wrong thing by going to Alaska for several weeks that fall. When I returned home, what limited hunting time I had for birds I shared with Macbeth and a three-year-old yellow Lab named Holly. The reason was simple: They were far more pleasant to hunt behind. It's easy to kennel—rather than correct—a dog with delinquent behavior, such as chasing deer, when you have tractable, eager-to-please recruits waiting in the wings. So Chaucer didn't get much hunting experience his second year. Out of guilt, I kept him on as part of the team. *Besides*, I reassured myself, *he's a slow-to-mature male. He'll come into his own next year.*

Sure he would. The next fall found me chasing quail in many states. During one stretch, Chaucer got to hunt twenty-seven consecutive days. He thanked me by embarrassing me over and over—pissing on a friend's pantleg in Kansas, rolling in cattle manure in Iowa, chasing Oklahoma whitetails, Nebraska pronghorns, and Arizona jackrabbits beyond the horizon.

Also, in Arizona he ran into teddy bear cholla, a type of spring-loaded cacti that is especially nasty. Chaucer bit at his assailant, and we lost a half-day of hunting removing spines from his face, palate, and hind quarters where his legs were pinned together. Then, in New Mexico, he was the only one of a half-dozen dogs that fell out of a beat-up old pickup.

But like some of the delinquent high school students I had attempted to teach in another life, Chaucer had shown flashes of promise, offering just enough incentive to keep me from shipping him out. In Nevada, he held a long point on a covey of valley quail he nailed in some grease brush and actually retrieved one of the birds I shot. In Missouri, our gunfire brought him back from a long deer chase, and he teamed up with Macbeth to give me the only double point I would ever know with the pair. Back home, he pointed a late-season woodcock although he refused to deliver the bird to hand. Wouldn't even pick it up. *At least he found the bird*, I thought to myself.

He might have turned into a good-enough dog had I been able to keep him in the house. Who knows? Other problems crept in—growling at the UPS driver, trashing my truck when I left him alone for an hour, nipping me when I accidentally awoke him. He got hit by a car in a freak accident when he refused to kennel in my trailer, running straight into traffic instead. Another time he ran off and was gone for two days.

Although I still have a soft spot for underdogs, I no longer have the luxury of time to correct their deficiencies. Each new bird dog gets the benefits of obedience training, yard work, and at least

A Fall of Woodcock

two months of professional training. Then they get a hunting season with me. Although I love them all, and although parting is such sweet sorrow, as the poet says, those that make the grade are invited to stay on. The others are sent packing to good homes where they can please their new owners in ways other than as gun dogs.

I began hunting grouse and woodcock in earnest in the early 1970s. Coincidentally, the first good dog I paid decent money for was a setter named Brinka, a daughter of the legendary Jettrain, whom I bought in 1976. But it was Brinka's daughter, Macbeth, who filled my heart with pride, then incalculable sadness when I lost her at nearly eight years old. Macbeth taught me how to hunt woodcock by showing me the secret places where they lived—those little niches of microhabitat within the broader cover. She talked to me with limpid brown eyes full of passion and intelligence. She made me realize how uneducated we owners sometimes are.

Returning from a week-long bird hunt in North Dakota one November afternoon, I felt sorry for Macbeth, who had to stay home because of airline regulations regarding too-cold weather and the transportation of dogs in cargo bays. So I pulled my hunting clothes from the duffel bag, put Macbeth in the truck cab with me, and drove to a nearby woodcock covert that I hoped still held migrants.

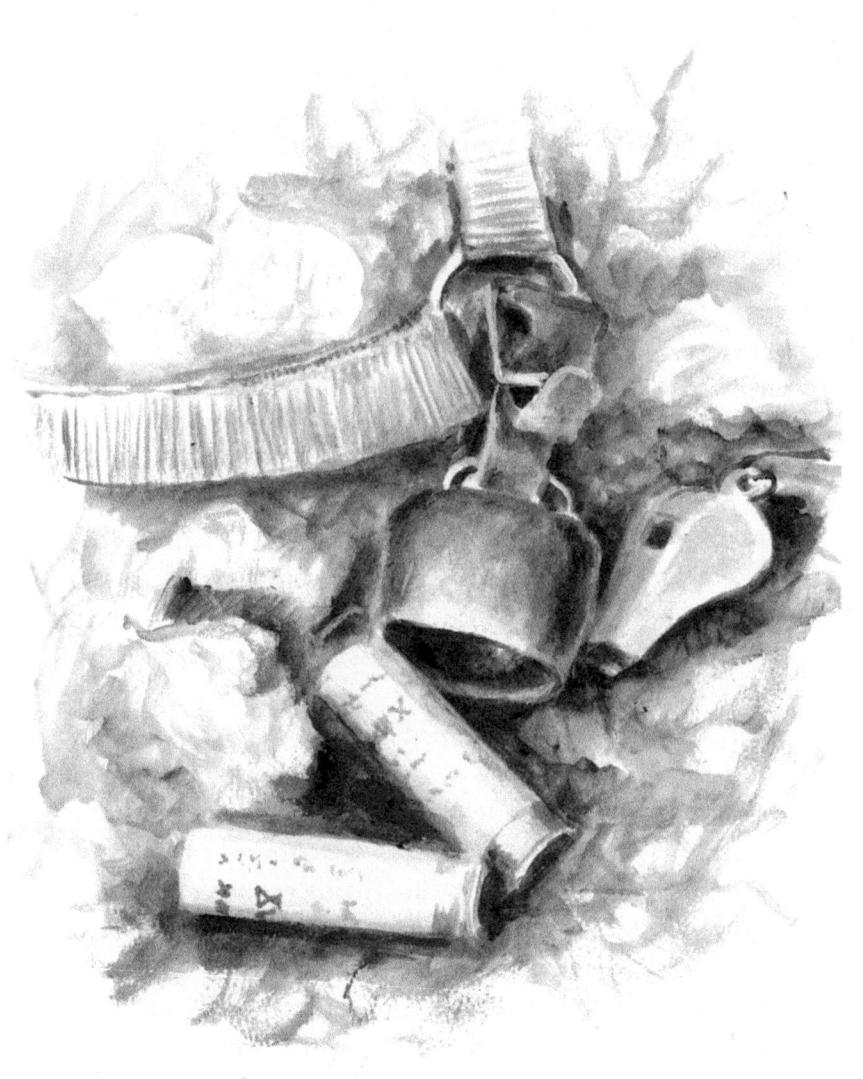

A Fall of Woodcock

It did. But Macbeth behaved poorly. She ran off to hunt on her own, flushed wild, and refused to retrieve the only woodcock I shot. I was so angry I ran her down, clipped a leash to her collar, and marched her straight back to the truck. "I did this for you, not me!" I scolded while my dog squirmed into her corner of the truck cab and refused to meet my glare. Still annoyed, and mightily confused, I drove home.

After a bit, I softened and extended the warm hand of truce. Macbeth stretched her lovely white head, flicked her black-ticked ears, and proceeded to sniff my trousers. Wrinkling her lips in disgust, she shrank back to her corner. The illumination was instant, and it was powerful: My God, I still carried the odors of Dakota prairie and sharp-tailed grouse, along with the smells of strange dogs whose names I had already forgotten. How insensitive we often are!

As a hard-core bird hunter, I know all about the thrill of hunting with well-trained, intelligent dogs, whether they belong to me or to someone else. A friend of mine has a setter that found my friend's glove two weeks after he lost it in grouse and woodcock habitat. Not only did the dog find the glove, all encrusted with ice and snow, he brought it back. I also know about the heartburn that even good dogs can produce when they mess up, something that happens occasionally with the best of them. I know, too well, about the heartache all dogs cause when they grow old, get stolen, or die. When these things happen, I wonder why I bother to own hunting dogs at all. I mean, dogless hunters don't have to bury their friends, at least not the four-footed kind.

There is a reason why dogs don't live very long, but I do not know what the reason is. I just know that five years or so, which is the average length of time that canine maturity and experience transect with prime age, is far too short an interval.

A Kansas friend of mine who hunts with Labrador retrievers figured this out many years ago. So whenever his youngest dog turns five, he starts over with a puppy. When I hunted with him one recent November, his Labs were aged twelve, seven, and two. For him, the inevitable is always somewhat predictable, and it is much less painful than trying to fill a void with more emptiness.

Every dog I have ever owned has helped me not only to understand bird behavior but to better understand myself. For many years I was a hard-charging hunter, so much so that friends joked about those "Huggler death marches" like they were a sentence of sorts. One particular woodcock covert—a thick mat of aspen bamboo they named the Hell Hole— turned aside all but the most daring. I still like to go into hard-to-reach places like that and I still wonder what's over the horizon, but I have slowed the pace considerably.

Holly, my old Lab, was a big reason. As she aged, Holly slowed down, which forced me to walk more deliberately too. One hot October afternoon, I pulled into a small clearcut of aspen, which was springing back with new cover. I wasn't so much interested in hunting—at least not too hard in the heat—as I was to let the dogs out for a bit of exercise. Naturally, though, I carried my gun. Fagin, a three-year-old male setter who was first out of the box, ran hard, looking for birds. He found none. Replacing him with Holly, I thought we'd take a leisurely stroll through the same covert and almost left my gun in the truck. Covering perhaps one-fourth of the habitat in the same amount of time, Holly plodded along in her methodical, old-woman way. She found four woodcock and I shot two of them.

She is one of only two dogs I've ever had to put to sleep, an incredible statistic, it seems to me, considering all the dogs that have shared my life. I buried Holly under an enormous beech tree along the hardwood ridge behind the house. I *figured* I had chosen the right spot when Laura, my wife, flushed a ruffed grouse from the beech one evening less than a week later. I *knew* the spot was perfect when Fagin pointed a woodcock in the lowland tangle below the beech and less than a hundred feet from where Holly rests.

I shot this woodcock, a young male. It is the only bird I have killed on our twenty-seven acres although grouse drum and pheasants crow from throughout. Buried next to Holly is Fagin himself, who developed an idiopathic condition at age four—

just as he was becoming a true birdfinder—and had to be euthanized by my vet. I visit both dogs often, in my mind and during daily walks to a little writing shack Laura and I call the Pout House.

It's back there in the woods, right where it ought to be.

3

NEW ENGLAND

Why are the world's great explorers nearly always men? One theory, according to a psychoanalyst I know, is that about the time infants are old enough to notice a physical difference from their mothers, they are denied access to their mothers' bodies (nursing ceases; Mother begins to cover herself). Many boys, and to some extent girls, too, develop a keen curiosity, which can lead to a lifelong quest for knowledge. The theory suggests that invention and discovery are a sublimation of the sex drive with its twin mysterious attendants—pleasure and power. It further helps explain why, since the recording of Western history at least, men have sought fountains of youth and dark continents. Had the bellicose Cortes not been torn from the breast at so tender an age, perhaps he would have spared the Aztec city of Tenochtitlan. Had Attila resolved his own oedipal conflict, maybe he would not have killed his brother and raped his way across the Roman Empire.

Who can say? What I do know is that my own wanderings are pretty tame. A coward at heart, I seek adventures through hunting birds in varied landscapes. Sometimes my wife, Laura, goes with me. But usually I travel alone because the success of any journey stems from the need to suspend myself, a condition gained through loneliness and long periods of silence. To accomplish this state, I must unhitch myself from everything in my life that is normal and habitual, orderly and predictable.

When you slip the moorings and set the vessel adrift, you are not unlike a woodcock easing its way south by degrees. And when the experience is over, renewed testosterone sends you home with the same urgency that male woodcock race north at winter's end.

I had long wanted to hunt woodcock in New England but always found it hard to leave bird-rich Michigan in October. Years earlier a continental journey for native grouse brought me to Vermont and New Hampshire in December when thermometer blood was barely readable, stuck as it was below zero, and when a blizzard blighted the woods. On another

New England

hunt in the Berkshire Mountains of western Massachusetts one November, I was too late for fall color and the woodcock had all moved out and on.

This time around, Laura and I want to see New England in all its autumnal glory, so we pack a borrowed motorhome with food, reading material, a portable computer, tool box (though my mechanical ability is limited to sharpening the correct end of pencils), two 28-gauge shotguns, a case of shells (optimism reigns!), boots, clothing, maps, cameras and film, and dog paraphernalia (food, whistles, leashes, chains, bowls, buckets, Frisbees, poop scoop, shock collar, bells, health certificates, and medical kit).

We leave home at 10:30 A.M. on October 4 after a delayed start due to paperwork, phone calls, and too many last-minute details. Three young dogs, each about a year old, accompany us in my old kennel trailer. The motorhome is a new 1995 twenty-three-foot Winnebago Brave, built on a Chevrolet chassis and powered by a 452-cubic-inch V-8 Chevy engine. It has tremendous comfort conveniences: generator, microwave, built-in coffee maker, TV outlet and antenna, shower, toilet, refrigerator with freezer, range and oven, lots of storage compartments, and sleeping quarters for six people. It holds forty gallons of fresh water and forty gallons of gasoline.

I wish the gas was as cheap as the water. I filled the Brave in Grand Rapids yesterday and now will replenish it in Port Huron before crossing the Bluewater Bridge to Sarnia, Ontario, where fuel costs

A Fall of Woodcock

another dollar per gallon. Efficiency appears to be only about seven miles per gallon but should improve after a few hundred miles. If I had remembered to pack a spare hose, I could hook it like a huge umbilical to the Citgo gasoline tanker truck in front of me on I-69. Where is he going? It doesn't matter—he's east-bound and he's apparently full enough not to miss a few hundred gallons.

We drive across Canada to Niagara Falls, decide not to take time to register the guns with U.S. Customs, and wheel into New York State enroute to I-90. Much later, at 10:30 to be exact, we shut down at a rest stop near Utica, twelve hours and 550 miles from home. With a trace of greasy Popeye fried chicken on my fingers, I shove ear plugs into place and fall immediately to sleep.

We awake at 6:45 to dogs shifting in their kennel. We are with the big boys now, White Freightliners and Peterbilts, their diesel engines throbbing at high idle, and they nearly touch each side of the motorhome. I wonder if my dogs are slowly being poisoned by carbon monoxide. Concerned, I let them out for a long run, then call my New Hampshire friend, Tim Leary, from the rest-stop telephone and roust him from bed. Tim offers sleepy directions: Highway 4 to Rutland, Vermont, then east and north on I-91. We will meet in the afternoon and hunt woodcock tomorrow.

New England

New England is an endless art festival. Vermont mountainsides boast an artist's palette of color; in the valley villages, white wooden churches are crisp as a Norman Rockwell painting. We pass parades of antique shops and debate whether to visit one of the many ongoing arts-and-craft fairs. Here is where southern New England (Connecticut, Massachusetts, Rhode Island) meets northern New England (Vermont, New Hampshire, Maine), or so the out-of-state license plates indicate on this October weekend. We cruise along streets lined with blazing maples and in our wake scatter like confetti thousands of red, yellow, and orange leaves against the curb and spill them up and over the gutter onto the sidewalks.

Stone walls (I called them "rock walls" until an elderly woman from Worchester, Massachusetts, who happened to be carrying a 20-gauge Purdey when we met in bird-hunting woods, upbraided me for my ignorance) march off on their own adventures. I note how the hundred-yard-wide highway slashes through forested mountains and wonder about cutting into history. In Rhode Island, and perhaps here, exist laws against disturbing three-hundred-year-old stone walls. What did the town fathers think when their descendants quartered and subdivided the land over and over?

The color we see on this bright, balmy day of Indian summer reminds me of northern Michigan—especially around the village of Honor near Traverse City, or the Cut River Bridge on U.S. 2 a few miles west of the Mackinac Bridge—but of course the hills here are much higher. The hardwood-covered slopes around Sugar Hill outside of Franconia, New Hampshire, are especially stunning. The town hall in the blazing sun at Sugar Hill is so white it hurts the eyes, and frost fires have deepened the yellow of maples to a burning amber. "Nothing gold can stay," wrote Robert Frost, who lived in Franconia and composed many of his most famous poems here. People can't always stay either, "in the derelict mountain villages of New England," as Edith Wharton described them, and so tourists, drawn to the fall color and attractions like The Frost Place, drive hard the local economies and have done so for years. In Twin Mountain, the sun-faded Seven Dwarfs Motel is evidence of a tourist trap that has been around since at least the 1950s.

According to Tim Leary, who meets us at Fransted Campground in Franconia at 4:30, one in every four trees in New Hampshire is a maple. Frosted peaks on the mile-high Presidential Range are from early snowfalls. They look like a bowl of sugar-coated Trix cereal. Tim says the color is two weeks past, but then he counts green among the array. To my eye, the color is at peak or perhaps slightly past. Apparently we bring good weather: Tim says the last two weeks have been overcast, with nine inches of rain absorbed so far. How could we know that later on this trip we will cry for moisture, and it will not rain again for nearly three weeks?

Leary, a freelance photographer and writer, has come home at age forty-five. Born in Illinois, he grew up in Connecticut, lived in Vermont and Rhode Island, and finally settled in New Hampshire. When we first met a few years earlier, I noticed he had a sharp resemblance to actor Tom Selleck, a fortuitous stroke of Fortune's pen which Tim has parlayed into free drinks at taverns where he isn't known and lots of moonstruck stares from beautiful women he would like to know. But Selleck, who grew up in Detroit, would never say "Come h'yea," to his dogs.

Leary received his education in economics at Franklin Marshall College in Lancaster, Pennsylvania. But under Tim's plaid woolen shirt beats a next-to-New England-Yankee heart. As a long-haired layabout in the early 1970s, he went to Europe for three months and visited fourteen countries on one hundred fifty dollars. His tactic, bred of a tight-fisted cleverness, was to order a cup of tea in neighborhood cafes. When the waiter asked what he wanted to eat, Tim explained that he had no money for food. Usually a free meal would follow.

But Tim is not stingy. Tomorrow he will share his favorite bird-hunting coverts among more than a hundred he claims in Vermont, and later we will visit some of the fifty or so he knows in New Hampshire. The ones on private land are only two to four acres in size, and none is larger than twenty acres. New England bird hunters fiercely guard their coverts against newcomers, swearing secrecy at all times.

A Fall of Woodcock

Best friends have been known to seal blood oaths of silence. The reason is that so few woodcock habitats are being made, and the mature ones left are in regression with only small-scale, selective cutting being done. One hundred years ago 85 percent of Vermont and New Hampshire was agricultural. Today, Vermont is about 85 percent wooded; New Hampshire 93.

Divide a rectangle into two triangles by drawing a line from northeast to southwest. The two parts of this picture puzzle, which, in reality, are separated by the Connecticut River, are Vermont (left side) and New Hampshire (right side). Otherwise, the states are as different as woodcock are to grouse. Vermont is all sedimentary—shale and slate and clay, with here and there a trace of marble. Some of the rivers—the Battenkill comes to mind—are silt-loaded and have mud bottoms in places. The Green Mountains, which run north and south, are mostly confined to southern Vermont. The state's northwest corner is part of the Lake Champlain valley. The Northeast Kingdom is a series of plateaus and rolling hills that are old mountains without peaks. Openings are underlain with fecund soil supporting the traces of old farms whose woodlots contain orchards with gone-to-seed wild apple trees. Hunting pressure is highest in the southern region although bird numbers are about the same throughout the state.

New Hampshire is home to freestone streams of polished granite. The imposing White Mountains, which occupy some 11 percent of the real estate, lie north of center. The big timber of this northern region is also interspersed with wild apples, a key grouse food in winter and attractant to woodcock, which probe for worms in the soft soil underneath. Most bird hunters focus efforts in the north, but there are lots of postage-stamp-sized coverts in the south, too.

"New Hampshire is very bony country, like a skinny woman" a friend and Granite State native once explained to me. "There is no padding over her bones, just thin topsoil. The soil in Vermont is ten times more productive." But the woodcock gunning is equally good.

Tim's live-in girlfriend, Donna Whitehill—whom Laura and I meet at dinner in town—tells us she knows exactly where Tim is hunting by the progression of gunfire on a Saturday afternoon around Franconia. A self-taught landscape architect, Donna is a lively and demonstrative blonde in her early forties and is the opposite of the taciturn Yankee. Donna's license plate reads LUPINE, her favorite flower. Tim's says PATRDGE, his favorite game bird. That's what he calls them, too.

I do not sleep well, thinking of next morning's hunt, and neither do my anxious dogs. Thrashing impatiently in their kennels, they awaken us at 5:30. I make coffee in the semidarkness and pack my hunting gear, then walk the dogs down to the Gale River where Varlet, the golden retriever, plunges in. I've

A Fall of Woodcock

never owned a dog that didn't live to shake itself dry in my presence. Back at the motorhome I change clothes, then sit on a picnic table, drinking coffee and watching the sun flood the misty peaks with warm butterscotch.

Shortly after seven Tim comes by with Ralph Stuart, a magazine editor and mutual friend from Camden, Maine. We hook my trailer to Ralph's old Dodge truck, a fading maroon pickup with crushed rear bumper and 114,000 miles on the odometer. Laura decides to stay in town and visit The Frost Place (unfortunately, it's closed). It feels good to be out of the motorhome and in a real hunting vehicle. Winding through the hills above Franconia, ears popping, I can see Mt. Washington, which at 6,200 feet is the tallest peak in New England and home to the world's strongest winds (measured, in 1937, at 232 miles per hour). And the Old Man of the Mountain, a humanlike face naturally formed by five ledges, which measures forty feet from chin to forehead. According to Daniel Webster, God hung a man on the mountain to show that here is where He made His likeness.

I wonder how many woodcock over thousands and thousands of years have winged south and back north again under this brooding visage of granite.

We are bound for Victory Bog, a forty-minute drive to the Northeast Kingdom and the widest part of Vermont. Victory Bog is one of the two most popular public hunting areas in the state (the other is Island Pond) with a reputation for woodcock and grouse. A North Concord stop at Copp's Biggest Little Store Around secures Ralph's and my nonresident hunting licenses. Copps has scores of baseball-style caps for sale, and years after the conflict itself, "We Won the War: Desert Storm" continues to be a good seller in conservative, Republican New England.

At Victory Bog I see the irony: How can a state so small produce a covert so huge? The elevation at the foot bridge near the parking lot is only 1,125 feet, but the seemingly endless wetland is so thick we cannot get a clear shot at the only woodcock we see nor at the single grouse we hear thundering away through the heavy foliage. After a sweaty morning of falling down and walking around wet tangles, we agree the woodcock in particular might be at higher, drier elevations.

Poplar Run is one of Tim's favorite coverts, and when we knock on that door, Ralph and I flanking each side of our host, birds are home. Tim's two-year-old setter, Tucker, stickpins something in a fringe of goldenrod that skirts the aspen canopy. A batlike bird suddenly twitters up and away, the sun holding for an instant on its peach-colored breast. The boom of Ralph's gun shatters the mountain silence. Feathers and aspen leaves, shimmering like gold coins, flutter to earth together, and the day's first offering is passed from Tucker to Tim to Ralph, who drops it in his game vest. The deposit makes a slight bulge.

A Fall of Woodcock

New England

I am happy for him and, soon enough, for myself. Tim's shout is followed by another woodcock that suddenly appears at the aspen edge, then presents a straightway shot and easy kill. I mentally pin the fall, and send Boo, my young shorthair who has been following me, in for the fetch. *Say whaaat?* Boo's lemon eyes widen in sudden alarm. I find the bird myself, a fat hen, and then tease Boo with it. On the third toss she picks up the woodcock and returns it to hand, shaking the bird like an old sock, and feigning aggression. My friends watch with keen interest.

"They're like kids in first grade," I explain. "Now that she knows what a book is, I can teach her to read."

"Your other dog, the golden retriever, ran off at the shot," Ralph announces. "She's lying down, scared to death, under that apple tree."

I acknowledge the problem. A month earlier, on Labor Day, I was sighting in a muzzleloader on my property when Varlet, who had somehow slipped from her kennel run, sneaked up behind me. At the gun's roar, she raced to the kennel and disappeared in her house. This was my year for young recruits, having lost my only pro, the four-year-old setter named Fagin, back in July to that strange condition which had several vets perplexed.

That left Sherlock, another setter and the third reliever who now waited his turn in the trailer turned bull pen, as my only Great White Hope.

A Fall of Woodcock

I often run two or more young dogs together, letting them get used to guns and feathers and the mosaic of odors and other scents from woods in seasonal transition. The best dogs sort out the hunting game mostly by themselves. The good ones usually need a bit of professional training on live birds in the off-season. Those that show no interest in hunting or that develop knotty problems like gun shyness are either sold at loss or given away. But all get equal opportunity to measure up.

Tim Leary owns another setter, Spiller, age nine, whom he hunts in small coverts for short periods of time. I remembered Spiller, a handsome double-eye-patch male, from our torturous, frozen hunt years earlier. Tim never puts out the pair together, believing that training one-on-one is the best policy because distractions are then eliminated. "Running two dogs together is like making a kid do his homework but allowing him to watch TV at the same time," he theorizes. The logic is certainly something to think about.

At Poplar Run we flush four more woodcock and three grouse, one of which Ralph kills with a spectacular shot through a brief opening in the aspens. At Woodcock Covert we rout ten more woodcock, thanks mostly to Spiller's classic points, but at least two birds are bumped by Sherlock, who smells them only after they have exited the damp covert. Back at the truck we empty our game bags of six woodcock and the single grouse, a fine gray-phase cock.

    We dine that evening at Tim and Donna's rented homestead, a sprawling two-story farmhouse with white clapboard siding, hardwood floors, and interior walls festooned with Donna's dried flowers and Tim's wildlife art. Tim prepares what he calls Woodcock Sauté. He sears thin slices of breast in olive oil, then removes the meat from the frying pan and sets it aside. Adding a little thyme to the oil, he crushes a few juniper berries for flavor, adds heavy cream, and reduces the sauce a bit before pouring it over the breast slices. Donna, meanwhile, has grilled marinated chicken, generously spread homemade pesto on bread, and baked stuffed manicotti shells with cheese. Everything disappears along with a couple bottles of California merlot. Dessert is apple pie à la mode.

    That night the exhausted dogs do not stir. The ache in my legs reminds me the proper way to read a landscape is always with your feet, never with an accelerator peddle. Just before falling asleep I think about a man named Norman Cone, whose personal history I began to uncover while strolling through a pioneer cemetery as a kid. In the 1840s Cone walked from Vermont to Michigan, claimed forty acres in the Stanley Settlement near Flint where I used to live, then walked back home to Vermont to collect his wife and belongings. Norman Cone's legs must have been tight as beech bark.

A Fall of Woodcock

Day after October day we awaken to skies over Franconia that are best described as Colorado blue. Looking up through the underbelly of a flaming maple, I spot migrating hawks high above and know there is a God and that He made days like this for bird hunters. The woodcock are mountain-skipping now, moving from covert to covert at 2,500 feet of altitude. Not every hide holds the needle-billed birds, but when we find them they are never alone. These are local woodcock, according to Tim, who awaits the migratory flights with the eagerness that others pray for the Red Sox to make the World Series. Typically the woodcock come, from God knows where, around October 16 to 21. The full-moon phase this month is the 18th. If woodcock migrate on a full moon, as John Alden Knight believed and others still think, Tim should have good gunning while we are taking our chances in Maine. I cannot say this phenomenon is always true, however. To my thinking, clear skies, favorable wind, and freezing temperatures are just as important, if not more critical, than moon phase.

Leary also believes that woodcock move up from alder runs, where they feed at night, to loaf along hardwood hillsides during the day. This, I agree, is possible. I know that woodcock move and feed during daylight hours, having shot several birds over the years with earthworms hanging from their bills like unsmoked Tiparillos.

New England

At Convicts' Demise, so named for the enormous rock pile it contains, we flush four ruffed grouse, one of which Ralph kills on a reflush. At the Town Garage Covert, we startle a pair of woodcock, and Ralph erases one bird over my head in a profuse stream of feathers. Our editor is shooting a 12-gauge over-under, apt firepower for a proper predator. Shells the size of Ball Park franks hang from a new quick-load vest he is field testing for some company. Ralph, in his early thirties, began hunting only a few years ago, and is in what those of us who have been there now safely call the "acquisition" stage of sport. I know of no gunner faster or more deadly on winged game, having once witnessed him drop, stone-dead, a pair of greater prairie chickens from the cold Kansas sky as they stroked by overhead at forty yards.

Monarch butterflies drift over a weed field at Convicts' Demise, unaware of the violence so recently erupted. Nature has tightened her grip on the trigger, but the butterflies seem to be in no hurry. Yesterday I saw a monarch drunk with frost, the milkweed field where I plucked him deserted of his travel companions. Autumn is supposed to be a time of urgency, the last rush of life for many living things. Is that why we hold off its knock-out punch as long as possible?

One day soon I will be fifty years old. This certainty weighs on the mind. What does it really mean to be a half-century old? It is surely beyond the euphemistic "middle age" (the few centenarians

A Fall of Woodcock

I ever knew are dead). Knowing we cannot cancel the inevitable, that the best we can do is hold it in abeyance for a little while more, we dye our hair, get a tummy tuck or breast implant, buy the latest copy of Penthouse, raise a new puppy. We should be glad, I suppose, that the ebbtide is part of a flow and not a sudden finality (if we are lucky). Octobers exist to remind us that all things of beauty must someday fade to black.

All about me are signs of this truth. A maple blushes red. His neighbor waxes yellow. Behind the pair a third tree glows pumpkin-orange, and yet the leafy lime-green undersides are proof that summer was here and will come again. Tomorrow this radiant beauty will shout pure orange, a blaze of glory from crown to ground. The day after, it will hold its breath no more, releasing the first of a thousand leaves.

A setter slides into an impossible point, stretching himself like a bowstring at full draw. The tension is unsustainable; breeding and training meet at the pinnacle. Like an ardent lover drunk with ecstasy, the inevitable climax must be savored, prolonged. Whoa, now. Whoa that point!

A butterfly begins its six-month-long journey south. A woodcock, quivering at dusk on rapid-fire wings, harkens to a silent, internal alarm. Is there any time to linger? Just one more day? The bird loiters and is found out the next morning by my young belled dog. Sherlock's comalike eye is transfixed on what he cannot see, but what his nose insists is canine cocaine wafting from the alders. Baby's first steps, and I am the proud parent once more.

It is an old alder run with mown strips to either side. The dog has twisted himself half into the ground, his ghostly form a bonelike blur in the shadows. Nose to ground, stretched like a white band of elastic, the feathering on his exclamation mark of a tail quivering. Spring-loaded. Unbearable. Something must happen. Something will happen. It is my call.

I shout for Tim to take the left, Ralph to cover the right, but they are too far and the dog too close to breaking. So I step ahead and flush the woodcock, which floats up through the clutching undergrowth on desperate wings, and I clap him silent with the right barrel of my 28-gauge double. Sherlock races to the bird and, squirming with delight, delivers to hand in a supreme moment of triumph. I don't know if Tim or Ralph or even Laura can fully appreciate this first point because they do not have children of their own.

The killing is at once the climax and the anticlimax, and the tang of gunpowder hangs in the alders. I ask Tim Leary the name of this local covert.

"I used to call it the Cow Pasture," he says soberly. Then laugh lines creep into his rugged face. "But I'm renaming it Tom's Gift."

Someone once wrote that Nature does not like a vacuum. Moments earlier and not twenty yards distant, we had heard a ruffed grouse drum. About this same time, Tim had discovered a spawning male brook trout in a step-across mountain stream. Guarding the nest of the skittish and now-deserted female, the male brookie sported fins edged with ivory and a throat of Sunkist orange. We could have caught him with bare hands—younger boys would have done so—but for us it was enough to witness yet another spectacle of fall without unduly disturbing it.

The odds of this trout living to seven-inch maturity are perhaps one in one million. The trout's tenacity for life makes us pause in wonder. The same is true with the woodcock. To hide from the dog, it chose the lush, green hell, stem density so thick I had to elbow the saplings aside to bring my gun to shoulder. And what of the explosive flush, designed to thwart four-legged and two-legged predator alike? "Does design govern in a thing so small?" the poet questioned of a moth, and I wonder now about a bird whose battering flight reminds me of a big-winged moth.

Question: Do I have this same intensity for living?

Answer: I don't know because something is happening to the gears of my body clock. I am aging, approaching the early stages of what people call the autumn of life. I certainly look fifty, and some would insist older yet. In the event of argument, a free issue of *Modern Maturity*, sent to every living American approaching the mid-century mark, waits in my post office box at home. Thank you, AARP, for confirming my fears in the same way my optometrist did five years earlier when he prescribed bifocals.

Physically, I am as strong as ever. I can walk ten miles, gun in hand and dog coursing in front. It is the emotional aging that has me concerned because I seem to be losing my predatory grip. I killed this woodcock for my dog, but he seemed not to appreciate it enough to pause in thanks before scrambling off to find another. Now I hold the bird and turn it over to admire its fragile beauty and for a moment I wish the bird had gone south. And then the hunter instinct is back as strong as ever. "Yes, go south, Bird, so I can find you and kill you there."

This is a bookmark I must visit again.

At noon at week's end we pull the motorhome from Fransted Campground and park it in a church parking lot across from Tim and Donna's where we lunch on hero sandwiches. The hunt this afternoon is brief. Tim must go to a Ruffed Grouse Society chapter meeting at a town in Vermont. He says no one will bother us in the parking lot, and if the police come tell them we're Leary house guests. Sugar Hill has two cops and both are named Dick. Memory jog: Two dicks named Dick. Got it.

Ralph, Laura, and I lounge in deck chairs outside the Brave, drinking cold beer and munching aged cheddar on crackers. Meanwhile, a roast from a caribou I killed a few weeks earlier in Ungava, simmers in the motorhome's oven. Evening shadows snuff the blaze from hazy hillsides in the slow-motion way a sleepy reader poofs a candle in the guest bedroom. The last honeybee gets its last sip of nectar from roadside asters. My hunting shirt, damp with afternoon sweat, now chills. A woodcock flits overhead, or was that a bat? No matter, it is the end of a perfect day.

Ralph departs for southern Vermont, and Laura and I are left to savor a red Bordeaux with our meal and to decipher the week's events and their meanings. A strange mutability is occurring in my life. Whether the turn is away or toward is not clear—perhaps I'm simply running in place—but a change has been launched nevertheless. The pattern has been to run and to gun, to suck out the marrow of life, then choke on the bone. Maybe it's to surrender to the experience of life and not push or act it through.

I recall Woody Hayes, Ohio State's legendary coach, admitting there were people smarter than he, but that no one could outwork him. That philosophy made sense to me as a young man. Now I wonder. Late in life Woody Hayes tarnished his reputation by ridiculous behavior—ripping up yard markers, slugging players, bitching at the impassive-faced officials. Defiant to the end. There's hope for another coach like Hayes. Indiana's Bobby Knight likes to fish and hunt birds, which may help to balance life's vagaries. Anyway, it appears to be working for me.

New England

On Saturday morning Tim generously leads me to one of his best coverts and suggests that I work Sherlock there, alone. It is a mown hayfield whose center is a dark seam of alders with tentacles that finger into the field. Sherlock points four woodcock and I kill two of them while Tim photographs. One of the birds runs, necessitating a refind and second point by Sherlock. I thought I had hit the bird on a right-to-left crossing shot. Tim isn't sure but he, too, saw the woodcock suddenly dive for the ground, a curious trait that snipe also exhibit at times. We walk to where the woodcock fell (or landed). Sherlock suddenly snaps to, and a bird flushes but I don't shoot because I don't want the potential of two dead woodcock on the ground in heavy cover with a rookie dog.

"There goes your bird," Tim says.

But my bird is dead, at our feet, in the same spot where the other just flushed. I wonder what the survivor thought when a dead comrade suddenly plummeted on top of him.

Later, we flush another woodcock four times but I cannot get a clear shot. The final exit sends the bird out over the pasture and into mature hardwoods that fringe the far side. I am happy with two birds bouncing in the game bag—one short of a New Hampshire limit—and I thank Tim for giving me the keys to his Cadillac. With a full tank of gas no less.

(4)

The Maritimes

You know you are a long way from home when ZIP codes begin with zero. My wife and I, with our three dogs in tow behind the Winnebago Brave, are bound for Fryeburg, Maine, via Highway 16 from New Hampshire. It is Sunday evening. The mountain villages are jammed with tourists on this most important business weekend of the year. Motels are full. Restaurant parking lots are jammed to overflowing. Between North Conroy and Conroy we merge into a traffic jam as tedious as those at the Pontiac Silverdome where fans drive recklessly after throwing things at the hapless Detroit Lions. According to the radio, Detroit has just lost, again, this time to

A Fall of Woodcock

the New England Patriots. A passerby spots my Michigan license plate and hollers, "Go Pats!"

I laugh and raise my hands in futility, but it is the traffic, not the Detroit Lions, that makes me impatient.

After the snarl clears, twenty minutes of open road turns into a crawl the final two miles into Fryeburg, site of the last and largest of Maine's regional fairs. An hour of idling in the dark, watching the red glow of taillights arc ahead of us where they disappear around a curve, prompts us to pull over at a roadside rest area. There I exercise, feed, and water the dogs while Laura prepares supper. We pop in ear plugs, then fall asleep to the slow hiss of tires on wet asphalt. Sometime in the night I awaken to silence and an empty road. Smiling, I return to a pleasant dream, the details of which I cannot remember.

We arise early and resume our penetration into Maine. Our destination is the Maritimes, specifically New Brunswick and Nova Scotia. Later we will return to Maine, and after Laura flies home from Bangor, I'll have the whole state to discover woodcock on my own. I had long wanted to visit the Maritimes, but the closest I had come was the summer of 1981 when my then-wife, Sandi, and I loaded our three teens into a tired old pickup, hitched a Scamp travel trailer (the little one, that looks like an egg on wheels), and headed out. If you've ever traveled and camped with teens on a budget, you know the money doesn't last long. We never made it

The Maritimes

to the Maritimes. Running low on funds about the time we hit the Maine coast, we blew what money remained on live lobsters and the L. L. Bean store.

I could look across the Bay of Fundy to Nova Scotia, but I couldn't go there. Now I could because the family had grown up and gone. More bird dogs occupied the interior places left empty, hunting seasons were open, and I had enough time to come into the country in the right way.

In New England we had averaged fifteen woodcock and six grouse flushes per day, but the 'cock were mostly locals, according to the friends we hunted with. Temperatures hit the low eighties by day and never went below forty at night. Black flies invaded the shine; mosquitoes droned in the shadows. But it was the Maritimes, where the coverts are huge, largely untouched, and reminiscent of New

England earlier in this century, that beckoned so strongly. If the flight birds were not yet in New England, perhaps they were held up in the Maritimes.

A leisurely drive along U.S. 1, the coastal route, brings us to Freeport a little before nine o'clock. A throng of faithful wait patiently for their local shrine to open. I'm told L. L. Bean will do a cool million in business today, and I do not doubt it. I recall stopping here in 1964 when the Bean outlet was a simple village drygoods and hardware store, and bargains could be found among the basement seconds. I bought an Injun Joe–type fishing hat of green felt for five dollars. Much had changed by 1981, when I last dropped in. A new two-story store surrounded by flags greeted me. I stood in a long queue, arms heaped with official Bean jeans and chamois shirts, the credit card twitching in my hand like a Mexican jumping bean. Laura agrees: We don't want to do battle with the Bean crowd on this precious October morning. We'll order from the catalog.

Maple leaves jaywalk across Highway 1 as we slip from town to town. We stop in Rockland for a long-awaited seafood dinner—knives and forks at the ready, plastic "slobster" bibs tied neatly around our necks like children demanding birthday cake and ice cream. At a hardware store in Camden I buy an extra leash and chain for the dogs and a galvanized ten-quart pail to cook lobsters in the Brave at some future time. Camden, home of Down East Publishing Co. where my friend and editor Ralph Stuart works, is without argument the loveliest New England town we have seen to date. Enormous homes soar above flaming maples that, single file, guard the sidewalks with solemn stature.

At Stockton Springs we pick up I-95 and drive at dusk through Bangor north to Howland, then east on Highway 6 to Topsfield where I stop for gas. Most of the six or seven people who live in Topsfield are in the service station, playing loud video games or waiting their turn. We are distressed to learn that the U.S. Customs at Orient, a few miles north, is closed for the evening. If I want to register my guns (and I do), we must drive north to Houlton, where the federal office is open twenty-four hours (Canadian customs, incidentally, at both locations never closes).

I call Danny Villaneuve at Hideaway Lodge near Canterbury, New Brunswick, and explain our predicament.

"No problem," Danny says cheerfully. "I'll give you the directions. You'll be here in a good hour."

How long is a good hour? Is it shorter than a bad hour? Either way, one hour is not possible because the distance is at least ninety miles. I have never met the French-Canadian Danny nor his brother Chuck, but I doubt that either has driven a motorhome in the black of night along the frost-heaved asphalt of unmarked and unpainted roads. Some three hours later, at eleven o'clock, we find the crossroads Danny had casually mentioned over

A Fall of Woodcock

the telephone. "We're a mile east, down the gravel road," he had said.

But at one mile there is no telltale sign of the lodge. Nor is there anything except woods for the next two miles.

Turning around the boxy Winnebago with its kennel caboose (which I can't see until it swings into view) on a skinny road is asking for trouble. I venture down one logging trail and can barely extract the rig from the soft ruts. Were it not for my wife, swinging our flashlight like some roundhouse yardman, I would have shut down right there. Back on the gravel road, we lumber west of the crossroads for two miles. Nothing. Suddenly, a provincial park looms out of nowhere. The campers of summer have all gone home, and the park is empty. A woodcock, momentarily struck blind by our bouncing headlights, hovers over a mud puddle, then catapults into the ink of night. We park the Brave in a tunnel of hardwoods where wet leaves press against the windows, kill the engine, and tend to the dogs.

We fall asleep to the patter of rain on the roof and the certainty that Hideaway Lodge has been aptly named.

Next morning we find it, three and one-half miles east of the crossroads, in time for breakfast. A grouse strutting across the driveway welcomes us just ahead of the Villaneuve brothers.

"We were ready to call out the RCMP," Chuck grins and offers a firm handshake. Then he turns serious. "We were getting a bit worried."

"Take Danny off the directions committee," I retort, "and your guests will have no problem."

"It's more than a good hour?" Danny asks with mock incredulity. "Farther than a good mile?"

The Villaneuves, who cater mostly to Italian and French clients, have been booked solid since taking over Hideaway Lodge in 1990. I had heard stories about their woodcock habitat-improvement program and wanted to see the results firsthand. Chuck agreed to squeeze us into their cramped schedule.

The brothers, who hail from Quebec City, live to hunt woodcock. Over breakfast, Chuck explains that because he and Danny grew tired of always having to hunt for suitable cover, they began to manage habitat on public land after consulting with and gaining the approval of the New Brunswick Department of Natural Resources. Like nearly everywhere else in the Northeast, alder groves have matured and openings have closed in with second-growth timber. No one harvests alder, and when they grow too mature, the supporting earth supposedly turns too acidic for good earthworm production.

Nowhere have I seen alder runs more dense and more extensive than in southern New Brunswick. They often skirt big farm fields, the way hedgerows do in England, and they typically line trout and salmon streams. Nearly impenetrable, they are often one hundred to two hundred yards wide. The Villaneuves use chain saws to remove dead and overly mature alders, then mow strips with a bush hog to create openings. A chipper cleans up the mess. Besides providing dancing grounds for males and nesting edge for hens, the strips make for easier hunting in fall.

Danny has a group of Italians to guide, and so Laura and I hunt with Chuck. As he drives us around in his old Suburban, which had logged 225,000 miles when the odometer died eighteen months earlier, Chuck explains their efforts. "Last year we managed three hundred acres," he says, "and have worked about five hundred acres this year. We hope to do even more next year."

Grouse and woodcock gunning can be phenomenal in New Brunswick when flight birds come in from the northern province, Quebec's Gaspe Peninsula, Labrador, and—according to some—Newfoundland. The Villaneuves' favorite covert sprawls over one hundred acres, but Chuck can't take us there because it is being hunted today. A few years ago his best day in this elysian field produced 101 flushes; Danny's finest day yielded 108 birds up. Anyone who hunts the long-billed bird knows that 100-flush days are the Holy Grail of woodcock hunting—heavily rumored, rarely (if ever) experienced. At home in Michigan, I have enjoyed 50-flush days, not counting birds I assumed were reflushes. But I don't do it every year, and, in truth, such days may occur years apart.

A Fall of Woodcock

On this sun-soaked morning in mid-October, the New Brunswick coverts are dry as a bleached-out chamois skin. Using my fingers, I dig into the alder ground and can feel no moisture. What little chalk is evident is mostly dry to the touch. Still, we manage to flush seventeen woodcock and eleven grouse. I kill a self-imposed four birds, half of the province's generous daily limit. I expend only eight shells, thanks mostly to Chuck and Danny's creative openings in the mature alders. My young setter, Sherlock, who only recently made his first point in New Hampshire, is equally efficient. We are becoming a good team.

Although Chuck carries no gun today, his passion for woodcock is infectious. "It's in my will," he tells Laura and me over a field lunch of smoked salmon, sea crackers, and aged cheddar, "that the wife will burn me, put me in a little bottle, and scatter me over a woodcock covert. Why would I want to be buried next to someone I don't like or don't know?"

Chuck has hunted European woodcock in France where he learned the French technique for preparing the trail (intestines). First, hang the whole birds by their feet for at least a couple days, then pluck and place them into a 450- to 500-degree F. oven for twelve to fifteen minutes. Next, remove the heart, liver, and trail. Mash these parts, after mixing in tiny slices of foie gras. Add a few drops of cognac to the pâté and spread it over a toasted baguette. Serve with a glass of strong Bordeaux.

"We're having it tonight," Chuck announces. "Of course, you'll join us?"

My stomach suddenly knots and I cough nervously. Although I admit to enjoying Camembert, Stilton, and other stinking cheeses (which are as full of active microbes as any bird's intestines), I confess to having never eaten the trail, mostly because I don't trust my unsupervised ability to prepare it properly. When I do screw up the courage, I'll likely follow directions from *A Thousand and One Recipes from the Austrian Kitchen*, by Josephine Bonné (1916). Called simply *Schnepfenbrot* (Woodcock Trail), the recipe calls for removing the insides and cutting everything into small pieces. Sauté diced onions and parsley in butter or chicken fat, add the insides, then salt and pepper to taste and mix with quartered slices of white bread. Put into a hot oven and bake until golden brown. I think I could handle that.

At day's end—a day Laura and I don't want to end—we thank Chuck for a superb introduction to Maritimes woodcock. Then we head south to Loon Bay Lodge across the Saint Croix River from Maine. Provincial law requires that all nonresidents hunt with a licensed guide, and so months earlier we had booked a couple days at the famous lodge. Loon Bay was built in 1935 by Richard Crooks, the Metropolitan Opera singer who was the Voice of Firestone. For years Crooks commuted by train to Loon Bay, eventually selling the lodge to former clients. The guest book contains well-known sportsmen, like Lee Wulff,

A Fall of Woodcock

Larry Koller, and Ted Williams, many of whom hunted there a half century ago.

Manager David Whittingham now hosts clients from all over North America. The rooms, which feature stone fireplaces and private bathrooms and are trimmed out in knotty pine, rent for reasonable rates, although hunting packages, which can include personal guides, naturally cost more. We stay in the room with the David Maass print of two woodcock flying through an apple tree—a good sign. The hunting season for woodcock is typically September 15 to November 15, and, as mentioned, the daily limit is eight birds. Ruffed grouse hunting season begins October 1 and ends in early December; the daily bag is six birds.

More than two hundred New Brunswick outfitters list grouse and woodcock among the game they offer, but only a handful are serious enough to employ good guides and dogs and to work at scouting areas of prime habitat. Besides Loon Bay Lodge, some of the better ones are Miramichi Inn, Old River Lodge, Miramichi Grey Rapids, Craig Lodge, Little Bald Peak Lodge, and Tobique & Serpentine. Many of these outfitters are situated along the continent's finest Atlantic salmon rivers, and so they offer combination hunting and fishing trips via canoe or tote road.

We hunt southwest New Brunswick in birdy-looking coverts, which again are devoid of flight woodcock although we flush a fair number of grouse during what we are told was an average production year. Typical half-day hunts produce a half-dozen flushes of each species. The problem, again, is a dearth of moisture plus unseasonably warm weather, which is holding up the migrants. Pointing out a thin stream of water spilling into Digdeguash Bay one morning, our guide tells us that normally the flow is a spectacular waterfall. "When I was married there, years ago, there was a torrent," he says. "Now there's not enough water to baptize a bastard."

The heavy rains that had inundated New England just before our visit spared the Maritimes, which have suffered one of the hottest, driest summers on record. Hunting the wettest places we can find, we flush occasional woodcock from stands of larch and tamarack, whose long, soft needles slip down my hunting shirt until they stick to the band of sweat along my back.

Evenings at the venerable lodge are spent sipping on a fine local Chablis called Jost Malagash, listening to Bruch's Scottish Fantasy violin concerto, dining on creative dishes of lobster and other fine food, and speculating aloud with the other guests when the woodcock will come down. I wonder how many other bird hunters over the past sixty years have sat before the fire and done the same thing in this same room.

Planning a woodcock hunting trip anywhere is a crap shoot because success depends on the

A Fall of Woodcock

weather and the fickleness of a nomadic bird whose brain is upside down. The process of deduction (Where are they now?) is fueled by reduction (Is the temperature falling? Have the leaves dropped?). Laura and I can't wait for woodcock, which are probably staging along the Miramichi and other great rivers of northern New Brunswick, and so we strike out for Nova Scotia. Our route takes us across southern New Brunswick, from Fredericton to Moncton, a pleasing stretch of farmland spliced with patches of birch, alder, poplar and pine, and immense fields of blueberries whose leaves are burning red. The few villages are only slightly populated, and many of the farms are abandoned with brush invading the fields, threaded here and there in turn with gray-black reaches of runaway alder.

Provincial law requires that landowners post their property with colored disks. Yellow signs mean hunting is permitted; red disks mean hunting is prohibited, even by the landowner himself. Most of the farms and woodlots we roll past sport yellow disks or are unposted, meaning they are open to hunting by anyone. Although many of the province's 725,000 people live in this southern region, they are spread out and very few hunt grouse and woodcock. For that matter, in all of Canada only about 100,000 woodcock are harvested each year, and 75 percent of that scant total are shot in Ontario and Quebec. The Maritimes provinces (tiny Prince Edward Island and

The Maritimes

Newfoundland-Labrador are the others) contribute the balance. By comparison, 400,000 American hunters killed an estimated 1.1 million woodcock in 1991.

What bird hunters live next door in Nova Scotia, population 900,000, also largely ignore woodcock, preferring instead to chase partridge. "Bird hunting with dogs in Nova Scotia is in its infancy," says Perry Munro, a native Master Guide with whom we hunt (as in New Brunswick, nonresidents must be accompanied by guides). Because I am running young dogs, two of which have yet to understand their purpose, Perry arranges for us to join George Hickox. Hickox, also a Master Guide, owns Grouse Wing Kennels and is well-known among field trialers for his champion springer spaniels. Both men are exuberant bird hunters.

Hickox, forty-nine, grew up in South Carolina and Alabama, spent his boyhood summers on Prince Edward Island, and finally moved to Nova Scotia from New Hampshire about seven years ago. Scrapping a successful commercial photography business, he took up the risky and punishing game of field trialing, which I'm convinced can peel a few days off a man's life clock. At the time we meet, George's charges have won more than 150 ribbons in Oklahoma, Michigan, Maine, Connecticut, New York, Alabama, Ohio, Wisconsin, and throughout Canada. During the fall of 1992, one of Hickox's dogs placed in fourteen

A Fall of Woodcock

of fifteen Canadian trials from Alberta to the Maritimes. That year, and the year before, he was Canada's high-point winner.

The man knows dogs: besides raising and training springers, he has developed successful breeding programs for Labs and setters and has brought Elhew pointers into his all-star lineup, too. His kennel, located near Shubenacadie in the country outside Halifax, is an anomaly to local folks. While filling George's Suburban one day, a service station attendant noticed dogs in air freight kennels. "What do you hunt with them?" he wondered. "Bear?"

"They're bird dogs," George explained.

"Why would you want to hunt birds with dogs?"

"Because it's fun," George said. "Especially grouse and woodcock."

"What are them? What do they look like?"

Central Nova Scotia is everything I thought it would be. Small farms stitched together with brushlands and timbered tracts. Excellent grouse cover, promising woodcock habitat. Our guides show us more coverts than we can hunt in a dozen Octobers, and we enjoy field lunches, a Maritimes tradition, along inviting salmon rivers. But like the woodcock, the salmon are yet to come. The heat and drought follow us here, and our search for brown October continues. After several hours of tramping through boot-tripping cover one morning, a jaunt which produces nine woodcock flushes and a single grouse, Perry

Munro, who brings local color and great companionship to any hunt, bites into a Gravenstein apple, notes the juice running down his beard, and says, "Good. My mouth's as dry as a Presbyterian hymnal."

Were we concentrating on grouse, we would flush more of them during the few days Laura and I hunt. Grouse have cycled high in recent years, and we see several along road edges (something you don't see in heavily hunted areas) and often hear them flushing ahead of the dogs.

"When it's dry, go high, at least for woodcock," George advises, and sure enough, he had flushed upwards of twenty woodcock the week before our arrival while training his dogs in upland coverts. But few 'cock, no doubt all locals, are around when we march through their summer homes. Switching to lowland alder runs produces better, but the hunting is tough due to the massive size of the coverts, which are interwoven with shoulder-high, still-green goldenrod. If you could shoulder the gun, there is no place to shoot but at a wall of living greenery.

In one covert along the Musquadoboit River, the habitat is so dense I trip over my dog on point. Even though we flush several woodcock there, I never fire my gun because no target offers more than a twenty-foot-long shot, and these days I consider it a crime to blow apart a little bird at such close range (I confess, however, that my attitude and behavior as a young man were the exact opposite).

A Fall of Woodcock

Although many of us wish to paint the woodcock as an elitist uplander, he is not. There is no iambic cadence to woodcock hunting, such as we enjoy with pheasants, plains grouse, and even ruffed grouse along tote roads. Instead of measured steps, we stumble; in lieu of the determined walk, we detour. Putting down one foot securely does not necessarily mean the other foot will follow. So we back up, sidestep, and strain to push aside the fingerlike branches that grab and hold.

And regardless of how many long-billed little birds find their way into our game bags, we go back for more every chance we get.

The hard work of field trialing has George Hickox wanting to shift into raising, training, and selling gun dogs. I see his best in action—Swaps, the foundation sire for Grouse Wing Kennel's springer line; Teal, the Lab cornerstone; a five-month-old Elhew pointer, who makes his first find while I am there; and Jasper, the three-year-old I instantly favor because he is a bird-finding English setter, albeit a Llewellin. Careful, selective breeding using Bondhu and Wynd-em lines is followed by judicious culling to produce Grouse Wing Kennel Llewellins with medium bone structure and wide, thick skulls. This is the classic setter look that George demands and is the opposite of the collie-snouted dog he accuses many breeders of producing. Color is naturally white with Belton or tricolor ticking.

1986 RGS Stamp Print
by Jim Foote

Plate II

"Physically the Llewellin setter can't lift his tail because the base of the tail sits lower on the body," George explains. "My goal is to get back at least a forty-five degree tail. I want it stretched out enough to see the feathering."

"Yes," I readily agree. "And what do you look for in a gun dog?"

George peels off the requirements on his fingers: (1) a great nose and tremendous desire to hunt ("An arsenal on the end of his nose."); (2) biddability, a genuine eagerness to please, full of fire but not a rebel ("I don't want to have to look for an Allen wrench to fit the screws in his head"); (3) the physical confirmation to do the job and the desire to go along with it ("A big-hearted, hard-running dog that is always

under control"); (4) a great pet who is good with kids ("Anyone should be able to steal one of my dogs because they're so friendly.").

The price for such an animal?

"If he's finished and experienced, at least two years old, I'll sell him for three thousand to thirty-five hundred." Considering that Hickox has sold dogs for up to eight thousand apiece, that could be a bargain.

At the end of our stay, I ask George to assess my young dogs. He is honest and to the point: "The setter is a good one with lots of potential. The shorthair lacks confidence, likes birds but is afraid of them, and is going to need a lot of work. The golden retriever is afraid of guns and birds and, well, you know what to do with her."

So you don't always get what you pay for. Varlet, the golden, cost five hundred dollars and came with enough papers to open a land-contract office. Purchased for my wife as a house dog, she had been banned to the kennel for digging a hole in the wall of our mud room, ruining the floor, and eating door-trim boards as high as she could reach, a considerable distance. Her vandalism cost another half-grand. I told Laura I'd make a hunter out of her. I lied. We eventually sell Varlet for a hundred dollars to a young couple with kids, and she is happy living out her life's purpose.

Boudreaux, the shorthair, is a sweetheart who wants so hard to please but barks at her own shadow.

The Maritimes

I bought her as a four-month-old pup from a friend for four hundred and fifty dollars. I should have taken ownership earlier, given her the intense human bonding she apparently needed, and should not have hunted her so much with my precocious, take-charge setter. Later, a professional trainer will spend several months with Boo and shoot one hundred fifty birds over her to build desire and confidence. In the steady, plodding way of the German short-haired pointer, she has become a consistent birdfinder who holds solid points and makes flawless retrieves.

I bought Sherlock, my English setter, from a customer who came into an Orvis shop where I was giving a seminar on bird hunting. The guy had this perky setter pup under his arm. "I knew grouse and woodcock hunters would be here tonight," he said. "I've got too many dogs right now. Anyone here got an extra hundred and fifty bucks?" There were no takers. Afterwards, I held the twelve-week-old squirming pup and wondered if he could fill the spot left vacant by Fagin, who was fast becoming a star until his untimely death in July, about the time this pup was born.

"He points the wing and has a lot of enthusiasm," the owner said.

"He might be a bit rambunctious for me, though," I countered.

"Got another one out in the truck. He was sleeping and I didn't want to wake him up."

"That's the dog I want to see."

A Fall of Woodcock

I've always had an attraction for tricolored setters in the way that brunettes, regardless of skirt size, turn my head. The white pup had black ears and a freckled face that looked like someone had held a black paint brush in one hand, a brown brush in the other, and then flecked him all at once. The pup stretched in his portable kennel and yawned, and the maze of ticking changed shape.

I bought him on the spot, named him Sherlock, and three months later he pointed his first wild birds, a covey of Kansas bobwhites. Then I took him, along with the others, to hunting preserves the next spring. Late that summer Sherlock accompanied me on a caribou hunting trip to Ungava. My two friends and I packed shotguns and killed about fifty willow ptarmigan over the youngster, who was a year old. Now, two months later, he has discovered woodcock. By the time we return to Maine, I will turn down offers of six hundred, nine hundred, a thousand, and fifteen hundred dollars for him.

The more my friends think Sherlock is worth, the more I know I will never sell him.

Woodcock breed throughout Nova Scotia, but the biggest flights come from Cape Breton Island. The birds drift southwesterly through the Annapolis valley and stack up at Digby, Yarmouth, and other port towns before crossing the Bay of Fundy. Laura's scheduled flight home from Bangor does not give us enough time to wander north to Cape Breton Island, a postcard region of abandoned farms, stone walls, and wonderful bird hunting and salmon fishing. Any woodcock hunter knows that farms whose outbuildings are crumbling invite creeping, second-growth forest. On Cape Breton Island some 250,000 acres of cultivation in the 1950s was reduced to only 40,000 acres by the mid-1980s. According to my guides, flush rates on island grouse and woodcock average twenty-five to thirty-five birds per day.

In hindsight, we should have traveled to Cape Breton Island instead of trying to intercept flight birds mixed with locals in the middle of the province. The ideal return visit would occur in mid to late October, about what you would expect for a bird whose meanderings are often keyed to degrees of latitude. This time frame is similar to where I have found migrants along the forty-fifth parallel, whether the location is Alpena, Michigan, or Montreal, Quebec; Calais, Maine, or Halifax, Nova Scotia.

Study a map of eastern Canada and you will discover that the land mass is huge, the distances staggering. Quebec, the largest of the country's ten provinces, covers nearly 600,000 square miles (only Texas and Alaska are larger). The North Shore, which skirts the Gulf of Saint Lawrence, is as remote in places as the Far North, which leads to Ungava Bay and the Hudson Strait. Few woodcock, if any, nest that far north, probably because Canadian Shield bedrock does not serve up an abundance of worms. But woodcock do breed in the Gaspe Peninsula—

along the south shore of the St. Lawrence River—and in the North Shore region all the way to southern Labrador. Labrador, which boasts less than fifty miles of paved roads, is another sprawling chunk of real estate that is legally connected to the large island of Newfoundland. Together, the land masses are more than 405,000 square miles (bigger than Montana). God only knows how many woodcock are reared here or in New Brunswick (28,000 square miles) or Nova Scotia (21,400 square miles), but the potential is considerable.

Canada's smallest province is Prince Edward Island. Ten times smaller than Nova Scotia, PEI is plunked down in the southern Gulf of St. Lawrence where it straddles New Brunswick and Nova Scotia. Its 130,000 inhabitants are the least urbanized in all of Canada with less than 40 percent living in the smattering of villages or in Charlottetown, the capitol. Coyotes are the largest game animal, pastoral farms are cut with brushy thickets, and the eastern and western extremities are timbered with red spruce, balsam fir, sugar maple, and birch. A friend of mine who successfully hunts woodcock there says the season begins in late September and runs to early or mid December. Guides are not required, and the daily limit is eight birds.

December? For woodcock in Canada? "The best shooting comes late in the season when the leaves are gone," my friend explains. "Some years the hunting stays good right into December. Then the birds leave for New Brunswick, Nova Scotia, and the States."

This unsettling bit of news confirms that we are far too early for flight birds, at least this year. Then I remember that the best time to hunt woodcock at Cape May Jersey, several hundred miles south, is mid-November but that in some years the migrants don't show up until Thanksgiving or later. None of which matters to our little nomad. He will be where he is supposed to be when he decides to be there.

Our time allotted to Nova Scotia is too short. We consider lingering, in the manner of woodcock, then whisking ourselves via ferry across the Bay of Fundy from Digby to Saint John, New Brunswick. Instead, we retrace our route out of Nova Scotia to Moncton, then turn south on Highway 2 to Sussex where we pick up the Trans-Canada to Saint John. Laura weighs the merits of canceling her flight home tomorrow afternoon from Bangor but decides there is no alternative.

Enroute to Saint John, where we plan to overnight, we have been looking for live lobsters to buy for a celebration supper in the Brave. But there are no lobsters for sale, and the campgrounds we pass are closed for the season. Faring no better in Saint John, which we reach at dark, we elect to move on. An hour later Laura spots a sign for Cherry Tree Campground and we agree to shut down for the night, open or not. The place is as black as a cave's heart,

A Fall of Woodcock

the cold air as still as a barn silo on a winter night. But power and water are still available at the full-service site I ease into. Across the road is a party store; inside, a hand-written poster: "Live lobsters. No order too small." And a telephone number.

"I've pulled me traps," the man sleepily explains, the Scottish burr thick in his voice. "But, to be sure, I can bring you five one-pounders or a bit heavier. It'll be t'ick and t'in to get 'em, though. Gots to take the boat and go across the bay to me partner's."

"Well, it's pretty late. Sounds like you've turned in for the night."

"I don't mind," he says. "Is t'irty-five dollars too much? Canadian, of course."

My brain races to do the math—only four or five U.S. dollars per lobster. But deja vu sluices my memory cells when he says it will take him "a good harf-hour." The directions to his house down dirt roads in the black of night convince me not to try it with the motorhome.

"I'll bring 'em to you," he says, matter of factly. "Is five too many? D'eres just the two of you, eh?"

"Five will be just fine," I say and hang up, my tummy rumbling in anticipation of our good fortune.

Back at the campground, a pool of light from the Brave's window throws a yellow square on our picnic table, but it is too cold to eat outside. Inside, Laura is trying to heat water in the new galvanized pail I bought in Maine; however the biggest range burner appears to be too small. Putting a towel over the pail and adding a big handful of salt help, but the process is laborious. While waiting, I try out a friend's recipe for woodcock hors d'oeuvres:

First, slowly cook two thick slices of bacon in an iron skillet. While the bacon is frying, chop half of a small yellow onion (if Vidalia onions are not available, choose the flattest yellow onion possible because it will be the sweetest) and cube a couple of cherry tomatoes. Set aside. Then dissolve two beef bouillon cubes in a cup of water. Dry three woodcock breasts, dust with salt and pepper, and gently brown them in the grease as the bacon continues to fry. Because I love the little bird's legs, I fry them, too.

When the bacon is done but not crispy, take it out, turn up the heat, and splash in a snort or two of brandy. Scrape the skillet bottom while the alcohol burns off. Then turn down the heat; add a little bouillon, the breasts, and the onions; and cook slowly. Toss in a bay leaf and recharge as needed with bouillon to keep the mixture moist. When the breasts and legs appear tender to the fork, remove and set aside.

Now, turn up the heat, add the tomato, the rest of the bouillon and the bacon, which has been diced. Bring to a slight boil and add a few drops of Tabasco sauce. While the contents are reducing, separate the breast meat from the bones and cut into pieces lengthwise. Lower the heat, add the woodcock (including the deboned legs), and—to allow it to absorb the flavor of the sauce—cook the meat slowly to a hint of pink. If you like pepper, grind some over the finished product and serve on crackers.

My wife loves it when I get domestic like this.

At 10:30, just as the pail of water is building to a rolling boil, headlights knife through the deserted campground. Two pickup doors spring open, and Sheldon McCreary and his friend, Brett, quickly appear. I open the door, a whiff of cold air rushes in, and Sheldon, thirty-five or so, a big grin spreading over his sharp features, shows me five beautiful lobsters in a big plastic tub. They smell like the sea.

Sheldon reads my thoughts. "Dey ain't never tasted fresh water," he says, "and de're caught dis morning. T'ought you might need bibs and forks, too, so we brung some." Sheldon and Brett refuse a cold Molson, heartily accept the fifty-dollar bill I offer, and bid us "bone apptite." I feel like I owe them my life.

The crunch of driveway gravel merges to the hiss of lobsters going into the pail. We eat them all, accompanied by a crisp salad and French bread and fortified with a frigid bottle of Vouvray. Sitting there in my underwear, perspiring, butter running down my fingers, the elemental odor of salt pervasive in the heavy air, I note condensation streaming like tears down the Brave's windows. With a sudden pang, I realize how happy I am and how much I will miss my wife.

5

MAINE

"Take a knee," says our guide, Jeff Pratt, "it's too damn hot to hunt so hard all day. Lord, I wish we'd get some rain. It's been six weeks now."

E.T., Pratt's big, soft-footed Gordon setter, comes by and flops down between Joe Arnette and me. Joe, a freelance writer from Kennebunkport, favors springer spaniels, which he leaves in his truck today in deference to Jeff's and my pointers. Arnette and I have exchanged letters for years but never met until now. Driving west on our way to the airport in Bangor, Laura and I thought we passed Joe on Highway 9. He was eastbound to Woodland, near the border country with New Brunswick, and Jeff Pratt's home. Four hours later, after retracing his route, I

A Fall of Woodcock

would meet him there. From published photos, we recognized each other through the blur of windshield glass.

I sympathize with my Maine hosts, having been in the position of needing to produce birds so many times when I couldn't. Over two days of hunting Jeff's prime coverts, we flush eight woodcock and four ruffed grouse and put a single woodcock in the bag. The unseasonably warm, dry weather has held up the migrants, somewhere to the north. An all-too familiar story now, but it matters little to me. When the woodcock decide to filter south, my friends will be there to intercept them. And I will be somewhere else, finding woodcock on my own and thinking about them.

Pratt has been guiding for eighteen years, and I believe him when he says this fall is one of the toughest. "It's especially hard on the dogs," Jeff says, as we rest in the shade of a towering pine. Like nearly every woodcock lover I have ever met, Jeff's passion is centered on dogs. He believes the best ones always know the instant a bird is hit and wonders aloud now, as we catch our breath, if the sound of shot against a feathered body is different from patterns that strike trees or fall apart in pure air. Jeff breeds for setters that hunt with their heads up, until they strike scent, and then he wants them to track with their heads down. E.T. performs flawlessly, his black-and-tan form floating through the poplars, and I'm certain he finds every bird available. And he hunts close to the line of fire ("Dogs that leave their ZIP codes are of no use to me," Jeff insists).

You will know Woodland from five smokestacks etched against the morning sky. Georgia Pacific owns the chipping mill here, and huge semi tractors and trailers line up at the scale, waiting to weigh their loads so they can dump them into the processors. And you will identify Jeff Pratt's home from Tanbark Kennel stenciled across the leaning mailbox with the missing door. Woodsmoke greets you in the yard. Inside the white-framed farmhouse, the worn wooden floors creak, the odor of stew emanates from the kitchen, and hunting paraphernalia is scattered everywhere.

Joe and I spend our nights at Long Lake Camps, a traditional Maine hunting camp that dates to 1945 and is run by a friendly couple named Ed and Kyle Staples who live in nearby Princeton. Other hunting parties here are also struggling to find birds, and we compare notes over supper. Late at night, logging trucks rumble in the dark far away, and I hear pines sough in the wind outside our cabin. Just before dawn one morning, a loon medley erupts on the lake. I know it is time for the birds to gather and go.

I leave for home in the morning, though it will take the better part of ten days. Joe is going in the other direction, to Nova Scotia. We shake hands and wish each other good luck. I hang around for a couple more days, hunting in the area and visiting

A Fall of Woodcock

Moosehorn National Wildlife Refuge and wildlife biologist Greg Sepik, the nation's foremost woodcock researcher. Eventually, I hunt my way back toward Bangor, stopping to visit a fringe of promising cover that circles a gravel pit, and again to check out a slash of alders that accompanies a winding trout stream. At the gravel pit, Boo flushes a noisy grouse, which sends her back to me in a panic, and I hear a solitary woodcock exit along the river.

At Bangor I pick up U.S. 2, and remember a trip twenty years earlier that began in the West along this same highway when I took it up after coming down out of Glacier National Park. A true, transcontinental route, U.S. 2 starts north of Spokane, Washington, and ends at Houlton, Maine. After thousands of miles of travel spanning thirty years, I can say without equivocation that U.S. 2 is my own version of Route 66 to adventure.

If you, too, are an eastern man of the forests, you'll feel right at home in the big-timber country of Wenatchee, Washington; Bonners Ferry, Idaho; and Libby, Montana. Rolling east, the road makes an engineering hatchet chop to skirt the southern boundary of Glacier National Park, and then breaks into the Great Plains near Browning, home of the Blackfeet Indian Reservation. Hundreds of miles farther east the plains become forests again, and the stink of pulp, the roar of machinery and the plume of sawmill smoke follow the road: Cloquet, Minnesota; Escanaba, Michigan; Mexico, Maine.

Maine

I have noticed that the number of churches in lumbering towns along U.S. 2 closely approximates the number of bars.

Another observation is that Maine is the only state east of the Mississippi where two of every three pickups sport racked shotguns in the rear windows. Every small town has its licensed firearms dealer, and the gun shops are alive and well. If I needed a new firing pin, I'm sure I could find someone to make the repair.

I pop out the tape of Tchaikovsky's Symphony No. 5 that Laura was listening to and insert John Prine and the Lost Dogs Band. "Ain't hurtin' nobody. Ain't hurtin' no one."

Halloween is approaching, or so the prolificacy of yard art declares. A life-sized scarecrow is caught in an immense spider web crafted around an old hand pump on a front lawn. Witches ride brooms over porches. Ghosts dance from plum trees. Huge papier-mâché bats swing from awnings, and a bloodied man struggles in the hangman's noose. Now I know why Stephen King lives in Maine, his castle-like home in Bangor guarded by a wicked-looking fence of wrought-iron spears, posted every few feet with ever-vigilant gargoyles.

Entering New Hampshire along the Androscoggin River and the White Mountains, I am mildly shocked to learn the birches are stripped naked. Have the woodcock come and gone during my absence? No. Along a mountain slope in the national

A Fall of Woodcock

forest I kill two woodcock over Sherlock's points and a third bird that Boo bumps and then retrieves. Altogether, we flush six woodcock in close-enough proximity to suggest they are flight birds. At last!

The find helps Boo's confidence, but it is clear she is going to need the assistance of a professional trainer. Someone who has birds and time and experience. Boo is what you would call "high-strung," but her hyperactivity is a symptom of mistrust, which itself suggests fear. Little things easily set her off. For example, one evening I shut down along a U.S. 2 turnout next to a small river near Concord, Vermont. Night has fallen quickly on this downcast day. I have already fed the dogs on chain leashes clipped to the trailer, and they are back in their warm, straw-filled beds. I have just built myself a generous drink and am cleaning birds in the little kitchen of the motorhome when two sets of headlights come flying into the clearing. The vehicles brake to a violent stop about thirty yards away.

Slamming doors. Loud voices. The unmistakable sound of an empty beer bottle rolling over gravel. Boo begins to growl, then bark.

"Shut up!" someone hollers at my dog.

My mind races ahead to the possibilities. My stomach begins to sink from fear. Boo responds with another volley of loud, vicious barking.

"Shut that goddamn dog up! Right now!"

Heart pumping violently, I come out with a flashlight and quiet Boo in a low voice while picking up the chains, locking compartments. I'm thinking ahead, ready for flight if necessary. I don't know how many there are, can't make them out against the glow of parking lights. But they don't know how many I am either. And they don't know what kind of nasty dog I have.

"There ain't no camping here, Buddy," the man challenges.

"I ain't camping!" I holler back, my gruff voice threatening indignation, not fear, although I am definitely trembling.

"Who are you? Where the hell are you from?"

I say nothing, return to the motorhome, reach in the door and snap off the light. Then I climb in and lock the door. My guns are put away. I can get them. Bird shot in a 28-gauge. I could fire a round in the air, then instantly realize how stupid that would be. Instead, I crawl behind the steering wheel, feel for ignition keys in the dark, and wait. I open the window a bit. No sound of gravel crunching under approaching boots. I hear low voices but can't make out their meanings. Two minutes. Three minutes. Finally, doors bang shut, engines turn over and catch, and the men drive away.

When I know they are long gone, I start the Brave (oh, the irony!) and return to Highway 2. Ten miles away I pull over at another rest stop. My drink still has ice in it, and my hand continues to shake while I stroke the soft ears of my troubled dog.

"Ain't hurtin' nobody. Ain't hurtin' no one."

A Fall of Woodcock

One of my favorite Canadian places is the Laurentian Mountains area just north of Montreal. The Laurentides, as they are often called, are among the world's oldest mountain chains and form the heart of the Canadian Shield, a massive bedrock formation scrubbed bare by Pleistocene glaciers. Woodcock live among the foothill forests of aspen, alder, maple, and pine. I pick up Siegfried Gagnon, a Montreal friend who lives in an apartment with his wife, Myriam, and young children, Hemingway and Emilie, in a downtown neighborhood. We drive to Laval, a northeast suburb, and meet Siegfried's friend, Michel Gelinas, who may be Quebec's most passionate woodcock hunter.

An electrician by trade, Michel hunts with a Braque Francais named Kim. The Braque Francais is a short-coated, dock-tailed pointer that some believe was the root stock for many of the modern, more popular pointing breeds. French texts that are three hundred years old mention the Braque, of which two types exist today: the Gascogne Braque Francais and the Pyrenees Braque Francais. The Gascogne strain is larger at twenty-two to twenty-seven inches tall and weighs from fifty-five to seventy pounds. Kim is a Pyrenees type, which range in height from $18^{1}/_{2}$ inches to 23 inches, and vary in weight from thirty-nine to fifty-five pounds. The brown-and-white Kim ranges close, has excellent stamina, and owns a friendly disposition. Like her master, she is a joy to hunt with.

M*AINE*

    Our forty-nine-year-old host is an intense man whose love affair with *la becasse* spans half his life. One of a relatively small number of Canadian banders, Michel has attached leg bands to some 150 chicks. The fall before I met him, he documented 190 points over Kim and saw 216 woodcock. I don't ask how many he killed because that detail is of no significance to either of us.

    The first time Michel hunted woodcock, he experienced *coup de foudres* (love at first sight) and has been a hard charger ever since. He hunts with a stopwatch (to document the exact duration between flushes) and a tape recorder (to capture the flavor of the hunt and to collect sundry observations). He shoots a 12-gauge French-made double with two triggers, an inge-

nious retractable sling, and 28-inch barrels, the right one of which is twisted (the French term is a rayé barrel).

During a rainy afternoon, we kill a handful of woodcock, each of which Michel carefully smells, claiming they have a mild perfume odor. Burying my nose in the breast of a large hen, I detect the faint odor of Pernod. Back in the motorhome I have no Pernod, but I do have a bottle of Rioja red, and we three towel our heads dry, discuss the controversy of full-moon migrations, and toast the Pyrenees for producing good wines and fine hunting dogs.

For me, a love affair with Quebec naturally begins—and often ends—in Montreal with its sidewalk cafes where you can watch the world's cultures stroll by and its wonderful restaurants featuring the world's cuisines. Montreal, which contains about one-fourth of Quebec's population of nearly 7 million people, is literally the crossroads of Old World and New World culture, language, and architecture. The French *joie de vivre* is aptly symbolized in this vibrant city.

I have been coming here for a long time. Ensconced in a Montreal-area motel in July of 1969, my wife, young son, and I watched Neil Armstrong walk on the moon while our black-and-white TV flickered. Like New Orleans, North America's other great French-speaking enclave, Montreal is a tolerant city. A few years later several fishing friends and I drew little attention as we raced through town one morning from our hotel to Dorval Airport. Sticking out from the cab windows, our black, plastic fishing rod holders looked like rocket launchers from the set of a Rambo movie.

Try that trick in New York and see if pedestrians don't dive for cover.

One area that always delights is Old Montreal with its busy wharves and streets, greystone buildings, and towering Notre-Dame Basilica in Gothic Revival. While dining in a posh restaurant like La Marée, served by vigilant waiters in tuxedoes, you can hear horses' hooves striking the cobblestones on the narrow streets outside and pretend you are in London or Paris. And if you are a shopper, lose yourself in the Faubourg, a Centre Ville warehouse converted to shops on St. Catherines Street.

A word about Montreal women: they are among the most refined and beautiful in the world. Besides their clear complexions, neatly cut and coifed hair, and contrasting outfits of black skirts, panty hose, and clumpy high heels—haute couture to the rest of the planet—they have a sense of dignity, self-worth, and importance. I believe this attitude stems from an early suffrage, a long history of feminine role models dating to Joan of Arc, and the freedom that comes from living in a cosmopolitan city whose roots are as old as Canada itself.

Siegfried and I return to his neighborhood late at night, and he offers to put me up on the couch. Instead, I choose to stand guard and sleep in the motorhome, parked on the narrow street below his apartment. His is a rough neighborhood with prostitutes displaying their wares under the corner street light, and strange people wandering about until the early morning hours.

Arising at quarter to five, I wash the sleep from my face with cold water. It is time to go home, and my motions are sparse and purposeful: nuke a mug of coffee in the microwave, hit the Brave's ignition switch, pull away from the curb. Montreal's streets are dark, deserted, and wet. Traffic lights double in the street puddles. By the time Siegfried is headed to his job at a government office, I'm already exchanging Highway 20 in western Quebec for the 401 of eastern Ontario.

All day I feel the drone of tires through the soles of my tennis shoes. I have a month's worth of experiences to sort through, relive, and tuck away in the memory files of my mind. All journeys have a purpose even if we don't always understand what the purpose is. What I do know with an odd clarity is that the stirrings that precipitated flight are satisfied, for now. Like my quarry, I am content to have wandered far and am eager to be going home once more.

Cornwall, where acres of sunflowers bend heads on thin necks to the east like thousands of Moslems at prayer. Kingston, where a speeding ambulance roars by to scatter vehicles like grain-elevator pigeons before the neighborhood hawk. Toronto, where no one drives under eighty, much to the joy of the Ontario Provincial Police (the opp cops) whose patrol cars pulsate blue and red while officers write tickets along the road shoulder. I know the drill so well: Kitchener, London, Sarnia, where I debate whether to spend the night, then hunt woodcock tomorrow on the farm of a family I know in southern Ontario.

"You've ranged far enough," Laura says over the phone, as darkness envelopes the highway rest stop. "Come home."

Home? I cross the Bluewater Bridge and touch down again in Port Huron, Michigan, where a stripped Camaro, its mag wheels missing, lies stranded along I-94. An ex-wife lives in Port Huron. Another lives in Flint near one of the General Motors plants, where I toiled as a press-metal production worker in another life. I slip past these ghosts in the night, then it's on to Lansing where my two grown children live. And a little farther yet, to the place I now call home.

6

A 28-Gauge Tribute

A time in your life will occur when you will shoot uncommonly well. Try as you might, you may not be able to recreate such success, and for years afterward all efforts will pale by your day (or season, if you are uncommonly lucky) in the sun. I don't know for certain why this phenomenon is true for most bird hunters. I suspect it has to do with confidence, hand-eye coordination, practice, gun fit, and luck.

I have been more fortunate than most because after thirty-some years of mediocre skill, I am shooting well again now that I'm heading into my fifties. The last time anyone considered me a threat to game, I was a teenager armed with that Mossberg 20-gauge three-shot, bolt-action—not exactly the firearm of choice among discerning shooters. My new-found prowess on pheasants, quail, grouse, and woodcock has nothing to do with the local trap and skeet league. I don't belong nor do I shoot sporting clays more often than once or twice each year. I certainly don't get on the birds as quickly as I used to, and I don't swing a gun as fast now as I did then. So, what is going on?

The gun is the main reason. My favorite gun these days is a Classic Doubles International remake of the Winchester Model 101 over-under. It's a 28-gauge and it shoots little shells that look like fat crayons. Little shells that throw less than an ounce of shot. How could my shooting eye, long given up for good, have returned so dramatically with such an underrated gun?

Isn't the 28-gauge dangerously close to the .410, and isn't it suitable for eighth-graders and delicate women? At first, my hunting companions laughed whenever they heard my little gun going off. Now, two of them have also converted to the 28, at least for woodcock shooting, and two others are considering the switch.

A hundred and more years ago, some English shooters also called the 28-bore a "popgun," a "little toy," and a "squirt of a gun." Others, though, writing in *The Field* and *The Rod & Gun*, praised its lightness, elegance, and effectiveness. Even so, were the 28-gauge not required in registered skeet matches today, it wouldn't exist and a score of companies

A 28-Gauge Tribute

around the world wouldn't make it. And if it didn't exist, I would probably continue to shoot 20-gauge over-unders and side-by-sides, and I would keep adding plenty of shotshell hulls to my pockets and the odd game bird to my hunting coat.

    Instead, I've discovered a whole new world of shooting by evolving to the 28-gauge. Nor am I alone because the 28 is beginning to enjoy a revival of sorts. Winchester, noting that more than four thousand 28-gauge guns were sold in the United States during a recent two-year period, now regularly produces the one-ounce load it carried as a non-stock item for thirty years. I use these shells, comparable to 20-gauge ballistics, on bigger birds like pheasants and prairie chickens although I compromise a bit on muzzle velocity (1,125 feet per second for the 28-gauge versus 1,220 fps for the 20-gauge).

When hunting woodcock, though, I shoot Winchester AA target loads, Federal Gold Medal sporting clays, or Remington skeet or sporting clays loads, all of which contain 2 drams of powder and ¾ ounce of shot with corresponding muzzle velocities of 1,200 fps. Preferred shot sizes are 7½, 8, 8½ (available from both Federal and Remington) or 9, depending on leaf density (finer shot strains better through heavy understories and canopies) and whether or not I'm in grouse habitat (bigger shot is better). As far as I know, the fastest 28-gauge shotshell available today is Remington's Express Extra Long Range loads (2¼ drams of powder, ¾ ounce of shot, Nos. 6 and 7½) with increased velocity to 1,295 fps. This added firepower is deadly on pheasants and late-season grouse but unnecessary for woodcock.

Of course you can always reload your own shells, something I did as a kid with Saturday-morning regularity. I must have put a few thousand rounds through that old Mossberg 20-gauge, which says something about the merits of practice, practice, practice.

I believe a slim, light 28-gauge is the perfect gun for shooting a small, fragile bird like the woodcock. My interest in the 28 has been evolutionary.

A 28-Gauge Tribute

About fifteen years ago I all but retired my 12-gauge Remington Model 870 pump and switched to over-unders with shorter, lighter barrels and drop-in choke tubes. Oh, I still use the 870, and sometimes a companion Model 1100 automatic, but mostly for waterfowling when I want that extra shell and know the gun will take a beating in the duck blind and boat. For wild turkeys I shoot a side-by-side L. C. Smith 12-gauge that my dad handed down. I appreciate fine double-barrel guns, too, and have even owned a few, but these days it is the 101 remake that invariably goes along with me on bird-hunting expeditions.

I like a raised-rib over-under in a gun I can lift quickly and on line, and one that I can lug all day. Over the years I borrowed, bought, sold, and swapped plenty of shotguns among my friends—in the same manner that we coveted each others' girlfriends—then settled on a 20-gauge Browning Citori Superlight, which weighs around six pounds. My scores improved with the lighter, faster-swinging gun, but I suspect the improvement had as much to with the fact that I was hunting more. One day while on a woodcock hunt near home, a friend kicked sand in my face with a deadly little 28-gauge Arrietta. He simply did not miss, even in thick broomstick aspen that required the kind of hand-eye coordination of a Nintendo master. His gun cost as much as my car. I could not afford to buy a gun like my friend's, but I could try the gauge.

A Fall of Woodcock

The Classic Doubles I settled on is built on a true 28-gauge frame, not on a heavier 20-gauge frame, which is the custom of many of the makers who produce the smaller guns. My slim Field Grade II weighs a scant 6½ pounds and comes with modified pistol grip and 28-inch barrels. Choke sizes are skeet, improved-cylinder, modified, and full. Besides its lovely American walnut stock and forearm, the gun sports deep checkering and just enough engraving to be handsome without being overbearing. A single selective trigger is adjustable. The gun has a smooth, sleek profile, the result of what the company—now out of business—called an "eyeball" cut, which is part of a series of extra sculpture cuts on the frame.

Others, much smarter than I about gun fit and ballistics, suggested that my good shooting was not because of the gauge but rather the gun. "It probably fits you like a glove," one friend insisted. I decided to find out. Like most American hunters, I had never been measured for proper gun fit, nor had I ever owned a custom-fitted gun. I paid $150 to an expert who figured out my personal measurements with the use of a try gun. Armed with that information, I asked another friend, who knows about these things, to measure my little over-under.

The drop at comb and heel were both within a quarter-inch of fit, and the length of pull and heel of pad were right on. The pistol grip fits my medium-size hand perfectly. A tall, fairly slim, right-handed shooter, I require a straight stock with no

A 28-Gauge Tribute

castoff. My 28 is straight as a ruler. The gun is balanced perfectly, too, at least according to the method described by W. W. Greener in *The Gun and Its Development* (first published in 1881, reprinted in 1988 by Chartwell Books). Held by a thin string, the 101 suspends at 2³/₄ inches from the breech, which is correct, according to its weight and barrel length.

I could not have gotten much closer to the perfect gun than if I had been custom-fitted after all. That revelation made me want to turn back the clock thirty-five years and measure my seventeen-year-old body, as well as the old Mossberg bolt-action that was so deadly in my hands then. We probably fit like dancing shoes on a ballerina.

Proper fit, therefore, is a big part of the answer to the question, "What makes a good shooter?" But it is not the whole answer. Knowing the pellet limitations of the 28-gauge loads, I consciously avoid taking low-percentage shots. I am also convinced that my ability to swing the gun without effort helps me to lift it quickly, getting it out in front of even the fastest-flying game birds, like chukar partridge and Mearns quail. Head shots kill game cleanly, even those tough ring-necked pheasants. I shudder now when I think back to the days when I either missed or crippled them with my 870 pump. That gun not only had a needlessly long thirty-inch barrel, but also sported a one-pound steel plug in the magazine. I couldn't have been more handicapped if I had tied one hand behind my back.

I have used the 28-gauge to kill nearly every species of North American upland game, including sage grouse. When a magazine reader saw that comment in print, he wrote a letter to the editor suggesting that I be "gut-shot" for preaching the merits of little gauges for big upland game. But I hold to my premise: In the hands of the discerning shooter, the 28-gauge will kill upland birds as efficiently as a 12, 16, or 20.

I believe, too, that the 28 is the ideal starter gun for women and youngsters, and it is well-suited for preserve hunting where the typical target is a close-flushing game-farm bird. The older I become, the more conscious I grow about toting unnecessary weight in field and woods, another clear advantage of owning a lighter, smaller-gauge gun.

A word about recoil: Even when shooting Winchester's one-ounce magnum loads, I never experience soreness in my shooting shoulder. The reason? Long ago, gunmakers developed a formula for the proportional weight of a gun to the weight of shot in the shell being fired from that gun. The formula is ninety-six to one. In other words, ninety-six ounces of gun (six pounds) should be able to handle a one-ounce load with minimum recoil. My 28-gauge 101 has a half-pound to spare. With a $^3/_4$-ounce standard load, the gun could weigh as little as $4^1/_2$ pounds.

The 28-bore has been around for much longer than many people think. Letters and articles in the English shooting journals of well over a century ago

A 28-Gauge Tribute

talked about the 28's supposed merits and shortcomings. It, along with the other bores, no doubt evolved from the English proofhouses, which date from more than three hundred years ago, as a way of sizing barrels. The introduction from France of pinfire breechloaders in the 1830s, and the 1861 patenting of the centerfire primer by C. H. Daw completed the evolution from muzzleloading charges to percussion cartridges. During this period, bores and chokes came under development and scrutiny.

The gauges, or bores, get their names from the number of lead balls required to make one pound. For example, twelve lead balls that are each .729 inch in diameter equal one pound, and that is why a 12-gauge gun has a bore diameter of .729 inch. A 28-gauge gun has a bore diameter of .550 inch because 28 lead balls of that size are needed to equal one pound. The bore diameters for 16- and 20-gauge guns are .662 and .615, respectively. The .410's bore, on the other hand, is already expressed in thousandths, as are the rifle bores.

The early English gunmakers made breechloading shotguns with various bore sizes. Besides the popular 12-, 16- and 20-bore barrels, 24, 28, 32 and other bores showed up. Greener, Powell, Macnaughton, Tranter, and Ford were among those who built 28-bore guns in the 1880s, and Ford in particular is credited with reintroducing the 28 after a period of absence. The earliest reference I can find to the 28 was in the July 1834 issue of *Sportsman*

Magazine. Then, as now, the 28-bore was a misfit of sorts and few shooters and hunters paid it any attention. Those who did, though, remarked as to its effectiveness. A *Rod & Gun* reader, writing under the pen name Priscus, in praising the 28-bore to good shots had this to say: "Their lightness recommends them; and, although they seem toylike, they afford as good sport, and fill the bag as well as larger and more cumbersome guns."

Another proponent of the little gauge wrote to say that his friends stopped making fun of it and admitted its genuineness when they saw the gun perform: "I don't pretend to be a dead shot, although a fair shot, and I can say that I find I make quite as good work with the 28 as I used to with my 12s, and can take my birds as clean and as far away with the little gun as I can with a 12."

And why not? Guns in 12-, 16-, 20- and 28-gauge are designed to throw the same-sized pattern at the same distances. Regardless of gauge, a full-choke gun is capable of placing 70 percent of its shot charge in a thirty-inch circle at forty yards. If the barrel is modified choke, 60 percent of the shot should fill the circle at forty yards. Improved-cylinder chokes will be 45 to 50 percent effective at that distance. Pattern densities will be thinner, however, with the smaller gauges, and that is why it takes a good shot to be successful at long distances.

It is also why I don't shoot a .410 at woodcock. There are 438 pellets of No. 9 shot in a stan-

A 28-Gauge Tribute

dard ¾-ounce 28-gauge load but only 292 pellets in a standard ½-ounce .410 load. That difference translates to one-third fewer pellets in the .410 shotshell. Consequently, shot strings are shorter and patterns less dense. In the hands of an expert (different from "capable") shooter, though, I readily admit the .410 can be deadly. A friend of mine shoots woodcock as well as anyone with a double-barrelled .410, the barrels of which he has whacked off to 18 inches. In Michigan 18-inch barrels and 26-inch overall length are the minimum standards for a shotgun. Anything shorter and the firearm must be registered as a pistol.

The bark of my friend's little gun is as loud as a 12-gauge, though, and I am very careful about getting ahead of him in a woodcock covert. The reason is that I worry about blown patterns that might send errant pellets my way. Too-wide patterns is also one of the reasons why I stopped using spreader loads of disk-shaped shot that were growing in popularity a few years ago. In my guns, at least, they crippled too many woodcock.

Besides less pattern density in the smaller gauges, the scantier powder charges make for less penetration of shot—a second good argument for passing up those long pokes. The tighter the bore, the longer the shot column in the shotshell itself (1.210 inches for a 28-gauge as compared with .690 inch for a 12-gauge gun). As the shot pellets exit, barrel scrub or friction is more pronounced in a smaller-gauge gun. Higher gas pressures and more shot deformation, especially those pellets at the back end, result. Despite these apparent deficiencies, the 28-gauge continues to perform well. The .410, however, does not.

"Balanced 28-gauge loads seem to do better than they should," says Mike Jordan, a Winchester ballistics expert. "Sometimes it defies explanation."

Those English gunmakers and proponents of the 28 discovered as much a hundred years ago, prompting one gun tester to write, "The remarkable shooting of this little gun has been a surprise to us, as we have no doubt it will be to many of our readers."

It certainly has been a surprise, and a delight, to me.

7

LOUISIANA

Early January, before the Christmas bills show up in the mail and a hint of mild depression has you lingering in bed, is the right time to leave home for a bird-hunting adventure. I should have started the heater on my old twenty-three-foot motorhome this dark morning when the thermometer is stuck at seventeen degrees and four inches of new snow has snuffed out the driveway. Michigan is sandwiched between storms. The one that strafed us yesterday saved most of its fury for Pennsylvania and New York. Tomorrow, its stronger sister will roar in from the Great Plains, where North Dakota is currently under siege. Let her rip. I'll be eight hundred miles south, hunting *le bec d'nuit*—snipe of the night, or woodcock—in sixty-degree weather.

Forty minutes from home and the motorhome still feels like a refrigerated meat truck. I half expect to turn around and see suspended sides of beef swaying in time to expressway expansion joints. The auxiliary battery is worn down to the point where the carbon monoxide alarm is beeping, which means I shouldn't turn on the propane. The engine heater will have to do the job, but will it? My shorthair, riding in the passenger seat, shivers, possibly from excitement, probably from the cold. Maybe I should have tucked her away with the two setters in the insulated trailer kennel.

Swirls of snow wander across I-69 like campfire smoke. At the Indiana state line, the truck finally warms and the shorthair sleeps. I run out of all traces of snow below Indianapolis, which I skirt, the cruise control set at sixty-five. The old rig is purring along, and there are plenty of gas stations to slake its raging thirst every two hundred miles. I take these opportunities to let the dogs relieve themselves and exchange turns riding with me. Louisville. Nashville. I no longer feel like running away from home because I am already long gone. The tether is elastic, though—it will pull me back but not until it is done drawing me ahead.

If you travel and there are birds on your agenda, you may understand.

LOUISIANA

Halfway through Tennessee, darkness falls and I decide to press on. In Alabama I can tell the terrain is hillier by the way the motorhome shifts gears on its own. The lights of Birmingham loom ahead. It is ten o'clock and I am seven hundred and forty miles from home. Where are the campgrounds? I fancy my credit card is still warm from being swiped through the last service station machine, so why not? I reward myself by checking into the Crown Sterling Suites Hotel, park my stegosaurus in an empty lot, and feed and bed down the dogs. The rib-steak dinner becomes a bowling ball in my stomach, a minor discomfort. I sleep the exhausted sleep of a new-sprung convict.

I was supposed to call Charley Sutton of Ferriday, Louisiana, but got to my motel room too late and Charley is no doubt out hunting now, when I awake, at nine-thirty in the morning. I'll call later today to arrange for tomorrow's hunt. Out in the trailer kennel, the dogs wonder if today is the day. Fagin, my senior setter at age three, shows his frustration while running through the roadside park outside the city. He snaps at the playful younger dogs—Sherlock, a six-month-old setter, and Boudreaux (Boo), a same-age shorthair. "Tomorrow," I promise Fagin. "You'll be the first one out of the box."

I head west, traveling off the interstate as much as possible to get a feel for the country, my

A Fall of Woodcock

first road trip to the Deep South. I am amazed at the amount of forest. The landscape looks much like the Midwest or New England. Trees are barren, a "hardwood haze" lines the horizon, and the colors are muted grays and browns with here and there a touch of green from pine and magnolia and perhaps tupelo. I wonder if woodcock live here.

Eutaw, Alabama, founded in 1838, according to the welcome sign. I drive around the town square, peopled here and there with curious townsfolk, mostly unemployed (I assume) men sitting on park benches and lounging around store fronts. I park the rig where I can see it from inside the county courthouse where I look for a tribute to the Confederacy.

From a northerner's perspective the South was, and is, a society of haves and have-nots. Ranch homes with two-car garages and satellite dishes in the yard dot the roadway. The houses are separated by clusters of tenant-farmer shacks where blue woodsmoke curls above shabby roofs even though the temperature is in the sixties. A forestry crew is thinning trees along the roadway median. Two young black workers shove branches into a shredder while a white foreman, arms folded, watches. Perhaps they would like to shred him, along with two hundred years of history? The entire work crew of twenty men in yellow hard hats is black; their supervisors are white.

Outside Eutaw is the Western Alabama Stockyard where auctions were held every Wednesday. Today, the building is boarded up with weeds reach-

ing inside between the warped gray planks. Next door is the Greene County Farmer's Cooperative, which is still open, or so the parked pickups suggest. A mile farther on I notice circling turkey vultures and then spot a half-dozen more trooping around the dining table, a bloated cow.

In Boligbee a few miles west, a pair or more of dead vultures lie along the red gravel of the road edge. I can't tell exactly how many birds because the carnage of feathers and wings all runs together. The evidence is indisputable: The buzzards were eating a road kill when they, in turn, became highway smears.

The black funereal robes of the turkey vultures wave as I blow by in the motorhome.

I press on, into Mississippi, and notice that drivers of oncoming vehicles half-raise in greeting a single finger off the steering wheel as we pass. I have observed this subtle sign of the lonely farmer-rancher along other rural backroads, most notably in Kansas and the Dakotas where a man may spend sixteen hours driving a combine and not see another person. Here, in Faulkner country, the bib overalls and stained seed-company caps suggest the drivers are farmers anyway. Chicken farmers. I motor past dozens of chicken farms, many owned by Rogers Poultry Company, whose long buildings resemble military barracks.

And cotton farmers. The picked fields are littered with tufts of raw cotton sticking from stalks like the exploded heads of milkweed in fall at home. The houses are worn and unkempt, surrounded by assorted junk and at least one burned-out car with sprung doors and a busted windshield. The cars are icons for the miniature landfill in nearly every yard. Wear it out. Drop it. Step over or walk around it. Endemic to poverty, the condition is not peculiar to Mississippi—I have seen similar neglect in Fairbanks neighborhoods, in inner-city Detroit where I was born, and in the low country of South Carolina.

LOUISIANA

At Pelahatchie, I cross the Pelahatchie River and wonder if this is the same bridge Billy Joe McAllister jumped from, or was that the Telahatchie Bridge?

In Forest, Mississippi, a black man with graying hair fills my motorhome with gas. Noticing the Michigan license plate, he says that he was born in Detroit. "Kilroy" in cursive red is sewn to the white patch above the pocket of his blue shirt. "How'd you like Detroit?" I wonder.

"Didn't," Kilroy says. "Ain't no jobs up there. So damn cold the wife took sick. When she passed, I come home. Long time now."

I think of the poet's line: "Home is where, when you have to go there, they have to take you in." In a way, I'm bound for home, although I've never seen it, never met the people who live there. C. L. "Charley" Sutton is a sixty-seven-year-old retiree of International Paper where he worked as a supervisor. We linked up by phone, then letter, on a referral from Stephen Pellessier of Lafayette, who had read one of my magazine articles on woodcock and contacted me. People should be careful about extending open-ended invitations—I, a stranger, have knocked on doors of well-meaning hosts in the middle of the night and startled them into recognizance. I would be knocking on Stephen Pellessier's door tonight except that his oil company job has taken him out of town. So he graciously passed me on to Charley Sutton.

A Fall of Woodcock

Near Jackson I take the Natchez Trace Pathway, a slow, beautiful drive through hardwoods and pine, all the way to Natchez where I cross the Mississippi into Louisiana.

Arriving in Ferriday about six in the evening, I cruise the town of two thousand people to get a fix on directions, spot the only motel—the Relax Inn—then swing into the service station for a taste of Exxon. The station is managed by a hefty woman with bad teeth. She is wearing yellow socks that match a yellow T-shirt and no shoes. The credit card machine is slow. "Cool socks," I say by way of easing the wait. Frown lines quickly reverse the glimmer of smile. *Fetish alert!* she could be thinking. "I cut my foot and cain't stay on these feet all day with shoes," she says, staring at me until heat flushes into my face.

From the pay phone I call Charley whose wife Camille answers with, "Where have you been? We've been worried to death about you!" I like Camille already. Charley comes on the line and I tell him I'll call from the motel after I check in and feed the dogs. But a few minutes later there is a pounding at my door, and the affable southerner heartily greets me in a loud voice that precedes the slight, stoop-shouldered man himself. Charley speaks slowly in a drawl that I have not heard before. Most of us who stammer a bit say "uh" between words but Charley says "owww" between words. Example:

"I, owww, gar-un-tee that y'all find some birds, Tom, but I cain't, owww, gar-un-tee how many." Or, "Camille's sister out of Baton, owww, Rouge, makes the best dad-gum gumbo, owww, out of anythin' that walks, crawls, or flies."

We leave the motorhome and trailer at the motel, and Charley takes me to Brocato's, a truck-stop diner where the food may be good but where the health department has not paid a visit since perhaps the Carter administration. In the men's room I decide my hands are cleaner than the fixtures and make a mental note to wash up at the motel. We get acquainted over a dining booth, Charley sipping black coffee while I devour two bowls of tasty gumbo, set afire with tincture of Tobasco.

At the Suttons I am greeted by Camille, a strikingly lovely woman with a full head of wavy silver hair. Camille gives me a robust hug; I know I am home now, at least for awhile. These are warm, giving people and I am lucky to be here. The house is old and cluttered, the furnishings worn. But it is warm and cheerful. By way of apology, Charley says they live how they live. I am grateful for being invited, and I am mindful of the old saying, "When you are in someone else's stable, you eat their hay." My immediate concern is two yapping Pomeranians (are there any other kind?). Looking like furred mitts, they remind me that I forgot to clean the windshield of the motorhome back at the Exxon station.

A Fall of Woodcock

Son Billy, age thirty-nine, and grandson Aaron, a twelve-year-old "gifted" twin according to Camille, show up after driving a half-hour to meet me, The Celebrity. I'm not at all comfortable with the feeling that I now must measure up somehow. To Camille I am a scholar because I have written books. To Charley and Billy I am an expert because of my broad bird-hunting experiences. They are not yet aware that I know nothing about woodcock in Louisiana. They, in fact, are the experts, averaging 150 kills per year. Already this hunting season they have pouched 135 woodcock for 459 flushes, a 30 percent kill-to-flush ratio.

In 1992-93 an estimated 11,800 hunters killed 103,800 woodcock, a poor year by Louisiana standards. Five years earlier some 38,000 hunters

bagged 300,000 birds. The annual harvest amounts to about 75 percent of the total take from the ten southernmost states in the birds' wintering range. Most Louisiana woodcock are produced on breeding grounds of the Central Flyway, west of the Appalachian Mountains, but some are also hatched east of there, or in what is known as the Atlantic Flyway. Makes one wonder if more than two hundred years ago the Cajun ancestors from Acadia followed Nova Scotia woodcock to Louisiana.

Louisiana overwinters more birds than anywhere else because of the Mississippi and its tributaries. Woodcock typically follow drainages as they drift south ahead of freezing weather, and one of the state's best regions is in the eastcentral area where the Atchafalaya and Red rivers close in on the Mississippi. The region takes in the northern part of America's largest swamp, the Atchafalaya River Basin (bigger than the Everglades), which runs roughly from Baton Rouge to Lafayette and includes the parishes of St. Martin, Iberville, St. Landry, and Pointe Coupee. Another outstanding area is the swath of farm fields edged with timber from Lafayette to Lake Charles north and west to the Texas border. A third area is north and east of Lake Pontchartrain north of New Orleans to Mississippi.

Since the feds cut out February hunting and reduced the season to sixty days, it typically has begun in Louisiana on the Saturday after Thanksgiving and has run through January 30. Hunting generally im-

A Fall of Woodcock

proves through January, but this year to date Charley's best day afield was December 12 when he and his party killed twenty-two birds for sixty-four flushes. December 18 was also memorable with twenty-one for forty. The worst day? One for two on the opener, November 27.

Because they drive so far to hunt—a hundred miles or so one way—the Suttons may spend only three hours in the woods. That works out to something like fifteen flushes per day or five flushes per hour on average. Because he is retired, Charley hunts about fifty days each year and only rarely runs into another hunter, another tidbit that has me hungry for morning.

In most hunting families it is fathers that introduce their sons or daughters to the sport. With respect to woodcock, the Suttons reversed the order. Billy's older brother, Bruce, first went woodcock hunting with a relative about ten years earlier. The experience fascinated Bruce, even though he killed only one bird for fifty-two shots with his Ruger Red Label ("Dammit, Ira," he told his uncle, "I don't think I can afford to do this again!"). Bruce introduced Billy, and eventually their father, who tagged along on his first hunt on New Year's Day when he was nearly sixty years old.

Charley explains: "I was dead with old age before I ever started hunting woodcock. I wouldn't even set in the same room with that oldest son when he and Billy were talking about "em. 'Till I went and found out what I was missing, it was all deer and coon and rabbits and quail."

I notice when Billy walks in the door he and his father hug each other, something, I subsequently learn, they started doing after burying years of bad blood between them. The feud was largely related to what Billy calls his "drugging" years, when he smoked marijuana every day. "If it wasn't for woodcock," Billy assures me, "me and Daddy still wouldn't be speaking."

"It was woodcock brought us back together," Charley agrees.

"We had thirty years of catching up to do," Billy adds. "There ain't never been a cross word between us since we started hunting woodcock."

Charley grins. "You tried to get me to go, but no way I wanted people talking 'bout me."

Aaron, Billy's gifted son, who has said nothing all evening, watches this verbal ping-pong exchange with intense interest.

At eleven o'clock Billy and Aaron squeeze Charley and Camille, shake hands with me, and prepare to leave. Tomorrow is Friday and Billy is visibly upset that he can't hunt with us, but he has to go to work at a marine dealership in nearby Jonesville where he repairs Yamaha engines. "Bubba won't like it if I take the day off," Billy moans, "but I'll hunt with y'all, Mister Tom, on Saturday."

Back at the Relax Inn my telephone is ringing. It is the receptionist, a Hispanic woman, telling me to shut down my dogs, which I had the foresight

A Fall of Woodcock

to lock in their trailer. "They bark for two hours and they do not stop," she complains. "People are calling here and you must make your dogs be quiet."

My mind flashes to the signs everywhere: "No dogs in the room." "Cash only." "Check-out time is 10:00 A.M. Sharp!" "Absolutely no cooking in this room." The kind of demands the owner of the only motel in town can make. I also recall Charley's recent insistence that I park the rig in his driveway the next couple of days and sleep in the house.

"Fine," I tell the woman. "I'll be up to get my money back and then I'll leave."

This maneuver takes her off her pins and there is sudden silence, then, "Oh, no. I can not do that," she says. "No refunds."

"Then I can't guarantee my dogs won't bark."

We leave it at that, but I sneak Fagin into the $28.95 room, mostly because his barking will keep me awake, too, and half-hope that he further soils the dirty carpet. I don't think he does, but it's hard to know for certain.

"Dammit, Camille, Tom and I are trying to hunt woodock in here," Charley humors his wife who is urging us to clean up the heaped platter of side pork and pancakes. The rich black coffee is cut with chicory and it is strong but not bitter because it is fresh and has been double-filtered. A couple days from now when I leave Ferriday, two bags of Com-

LOUISIANA

munity Roast will accompany me, along with a huge sack of shucked pecans "from our tree, right there in the front yard," Charley will point out with pride. I have experienced it before—the less some people have, the more they try to give away.

Another example: A week after returning home, I realize I have lost a special dog bell, one that I had bought years earlier from my grandfather's natal village in the Swiss Alps. Backtracking in my mind, I remembered removing it from Sherlock in the Brake by Bruce's, Charley's name for the last covert we hunted. Bruce, whom I meet briefly during my stay, lives one hundred miles from his parents, but that doesn't stop Charley from ringing him up and describing in detail where we parked and what the bell looks like. Four days later the UPS driver delivers it to me.

Charley doesn't have much and what he does own has been through the wringer. His hunting car, a 1981 beater of a station wagon, set him back six-hundred dollars when he bought it with 140,000 miles. The 1981 four-cylinder Datsun now has 201,000 miles and looks it. The cracked vinyl dashboard resembles the web of a drunken spider. Mounds of gear litter the back seat, and dust suffocates everything. Charley proudly allows that mechanic Billy has never had the valve cover off the original engine. "It gets good gas mileage," Charley admits, "but not as good as the old Subaru did. On one of our first trips me and Billy put 2,500 miles on that one over thirteen days of hunting and camping. We burned only a hundred gallons of gas."

Charley's dogs are fifty-dollar bargains—a half-Brittany, half-setter named Dot and another named Pete, a pair of year-old English pointers, setters Betty and, his favorite, BoJay's Gal. They are good dogs, as I will learn. Charley picks three from the backyard kennel and loads them to one side of his trailer, a homemade, low-slung box with six compartments. The trailer has a lift-top for storing more gear and a seat for changing boots. My dogs unwillingly go in the other side. Charley immediately falls in love with my young shorthair. "Her name's Boo," I explain. "Short for Boudreaux."

"That's a coonass dog, Tom," Charley laughs as he nuzzles the liver-colored Boo. "Half the dogs in Lose-ee-anner are named Boudreaux. Give you fifty dollars for her."

I'm learning that Charley always tacks an "er" to proper nouns ending in the letter "a." "Florida," for example, becomes "Florider." "Upper Peninsula" is "Upper Peninsuler."

State wildlife management areas offer some of the best woodcock gunning, but most are closed to bird hunting in early January because of the ongoing deer hunting season. So Charley and I head north toward Arkansas. Two hours later he pulls up to what he calls the Central Brake, a swatch of heavy

Louisiana

woods and brush flanked by cotton and bean fields. The day is balmy and bright; the frozen north seems a world away. We bell the dogs, load guns, and set out. Almost immediately, BoJay's Gal strikes a handsome point in a tangle of nearly impenetrable brush and a woodcock goes busting out the other side. Charley downs the bird with a single shot, but the cover is so thick I am unable to mark the fall. Charley does, and retrieves his kill—a fat hen.

Wherever I have found woodcock, three habitat conditions have always been evident. The first is fairly heavy stem density from an overstory of trees or other plants that may range to thirty feet in height and whose crowns provide some form of protective canopy. In Louisiana sweet gum, hackberry, and locust are common overstories, along with switch cane and an odd-looking weed locals call devil's walking stick. Picture giant ragweed with straight, paired thorns a half-inch long on the stalks.

The second key is an understory of brush, forbs, or other plants, which are usually alive but may be dead or leafless. In the Central Brake and other coverts we explore, Charley points out honeysuckle, blackberry, wax myrtle, gnarly masses of low-growing buck vine, and red haw or water privet, a plant that sports red berries and reminds me of holly back home.

The third requirement is that the ground must be open enough for woodcock to see and to run through. The best places are moist and contain dead leaves in a parklike environment. You will notice the color brown rather than green. The best brakes are often wet, either from rain or receding floodwaters.

Louisiana wildlife biologists back up my observations. Researchers have determined that woodcock use three broad types of habitat during daytime, namely lowland hardwood swamps, upland piney woods, and bay galls. Within these three types is a wide range of flora and structural characteristics, the most importance of which is that they reflect soil moisture and produce lots of earthworms. Wet soil and stem density create the dream fields we hope for.

During a limited study of radio-collared hens, researchers found that most of the birds (64 percent) favored daytime overstories of sycamore, sweetgum, and American elm, followed by hackberry, American elm, and ash (30 percent). Blackberry was the understory most frequented, followed closely by marsh fern, then seedlings/saplings, and blowdowns. Most hens stayed within a quarter-mile of where they were tagged in December, until late February when nearly all dispersed for northern breeding grounds.

From the highway, these southern woodcock haunts appear similar to those in northern coverts—

a furze of hardwoods skirted by a brushy understory. You won't know woodcock live there, though, unless you get out of the car and walk into the habitat. And when conditions are right, you will know it, even to the point of expecting the flush before your dog finds the bird. Is it a sixth sense? The mind's ability to reduce hundreds of covers, imagined or experienced, to those few that hold birds? I can't say, but I know that those woodcock hunters who thrill to the flush and who have enough experience to think of the kill as anticlimactic to the flush understand this phenomenon.

The critical difference between northern and southern habitats is that the latter demand that you wear seventeen-inch-high rubber boots, briar-proof chaps, and noninsulated gloves. At home I sometimes look at the few scratches and cuts on the backs of my hands—those stitch marks of experience—with a certain feeling of pride. In Louisiana, if you have failed to protect yourself, you will look at your lacerated and punctured body and feel pain.

Fagin pins a bird in a blowdown guarded by a wicked blackberry tangle. Fortunately, just as I decide on an angle to penetrate, the bird catapults up and away, down a tunnellike opening between trees. I shoot, he crumples, Fagin retrieves, and Charley says "Welcome to Lose-ee-anner!" We flush six woodcock in all and shoot four. Later that afternoon in some birdy-looking cover, Charley kills the only woodcock we flush.

"I thought if we threw a dog in there, we'd find lots of birds, but the weather's too warm," he apologizes. "I think most of them have moved out."

Whether or not Louisiana woodcock migrate back and forth all winter is the subject of much speculation. During cold snaps it is not uncommon to find them in the last fringes of upland habitat above the Gulf of Mexico because they have nowhere else to go. I have heard stories of woodcock starving to death during those infrequent times when portions of the Deep South freeze over. But a woodcock is mobile, and his wings take him to where food is most abundant. When winters are warm, many birds shortstop in Missouri or Kentucky. A frigid spell sends them to the next tier of states—Arkansas and Tennessee—and eventually, Louisiana, where thousands spill into the Atchafalaya Basin and other swamps. Charley believes when the weather is too warm, they'll move back north where the temperature is cooler. The limited radiotelemetry study, however, suggests that once they reach Louisiana they don't reverse-migrate until spring. More research is needed.

Hunters take very few, even in heavily pressured areas like the Atchafalaya National Wildlife Refuge and Sherburne Wildlife Management Area. Mandatory check-in at these public-hunting properties showed that in most years hunters harvested only one of every twenty birds banded. In 1994–95 when hunting was poor, they shot only 3 of 229 woodcock banded. If the cover there is as thick as the brakes that Charley and I hunted, I can understand this surprisingly low figure.

The next day Charley and I are joined by son Billy and Troy Temple, a landowner who lets us hunt near Crowville. We flush seven birds and kill two during a leisurely stroll. "We leave it up to the dogs," Charley explains when I ask the reason for the slow pace. "We don't tell them where to go or how fast to get there. Down here in summer we do everything slower to survive the heat and humidity. It just naturally carries over into winter."

"That's a good way to get lost," I suggest, thinking of northern Michigan's seemingly endless clearcuts—huge aspen slashings that can run for miles.

"Oh, we never get lost," Charley says. "The Yankees up north (anywhere above I-20, which runs west out of Vicksburg through Shreveport–Bossier City) know only four directions. Us coonasses know six. Even our women know up and down."

During frequent rest stops the subject is always woodcock. I note the Suttons use only No. 6 shot in their 20-gauge Churchill double barrels, cut down to twenty-three inches and bored skeet and skeet. The reason, claims Billy, who reloads, is better knock-down power. "We don't strain our shot through leaves like y'all do," he says. "We shoot through brush and timber. Check the muzzle-velocity statistics if you don't believe me. We used to shoot No. 9 shot in 12-gauge, then went to 8s and $7^1/_2$s and now 6s,

A Fall of Woodcock

crippling fewer and fewer birds as we went to bigger and bigger shot."

I learn that Charley and Billy are students of woodcock, reading everything they can find on the subject and constantly testing others' theories and coming up with their own. Billy says he knew a farmer who reported that while cutting cotton at night, he watched woodcock fly up from the field and hit the windshield of his tractor. Billy and his son, Aaron, checked it out. Using powerful mag lights, one night they stalked a picked field and saw woodcock, their eyes glowing red in the flashlight beam, strut down the rows, hunting for worms.

"Mister Tom, it's something else to see," the animated Billy says, suddenly jumping up to demonstrate. "They stop and cock their heads to listen, like this." He pauses to drop head to shoulder, eyes opening wide. "Then, they take one more step, like a pitcher coming off the mound, see. Pow! They stab that worm so fast you cain't hardly see it, just like a fastball going by in a blur."

Billy claims that a game warden he knows witnessed a woodcock walk completely around a tree trunk, gripping the bark several feet off the ground with its toes while searching for worms. Theory: When timber floods, worms are forced from the soil and climb trees to avoid being drowned.

"Don't that beat all?" Billy insists. "And I'll tell you something else. I believe a woodcock can crack acorns ("ache erns"). I saw a bird fly off one time, an acorn in its bill. I shot the bird and it died with the nut in its mouth. There's a tiny worm in some of them acorns..."

Much of what Billy believes he learned from Uncle Ira, a veteran woodcock hunter who also knows a lot about dogs. One day Billy was berating Dot, the half-setter, half-Brittany, for bringing back a box terrapin turtle. "Don't do that," Ira warned Billy. "The dog don't know no difference. A box terrapin smells exactly like a woodcock."

Ira also told Billy the only thing you can teach a dog is Whoa. "Everything else a dog learns is by experience," Ira said. "Ever notice how dead birds are harder to find than crippled birds? That's because dead birds don't breathe. A dog can smell a live bird's breath."

The afternoon and the next day pass all too quickly. The hunting is not as good as we had hoped for, but I learn many things and the Suttons are great hosts. Later, I will hunt snipe near Gueydan in sight of the Intracoastal Waterway; eat crawfish, snipe gumbo, and boudin (dirty rice and sausage stuffed in a casing); and see the Cajun side of multi-ethnic Louisiana. But that's another story. It was woodcock, including those northern birds I missed last fall, that brought me to Louisiana in the first place. Charley tells me I'm not the first Michigander to come down. Another friend of his, a Doc Stahl from Northville near Detroit, and his wife, Ann, leave their large-animal veterinary business for a few days each winter to hunt with the Suttons. One day Charley came upon the good doctor, who is stricken with lupus disease, sitting down and staring at a huge cypress that could have been five hundred years old.

"What's the matter?" Charley nervously wondered.

"Nothing," his friend said. "I was just thanking God for letting me live long enough to come down here to see this cypress tree."

Louisiana is one of a half-dozen states with no ruffed grouse, but the Ruffed Grouse Society is active here through its only Deep South chapter, the Cajun Becasse Society. The RGS put up $40,000 to go with $60,000 pledged by the U.S. Fish & Wildlife Service to study survival, movement, and habitat use of woodcock in southcentral Louisiana. The Cajun Becasse Society raises money at its annual banquet held near Opelousas in late January. I was disappointed that I would be back home, and probably freezing, when party time rolled around.

Yet somehow, on the eve of my departure, Charley has wrangled an invitation for us to visit an honest-to-God duck hunting camp on the other side of Jonesville near the Catahoula National Wildlife Refuge. Owned by Frank Harris III, who runs a geologic consulting business out of Shreveport, the lodge is amply furnished with limited-edition sporting art and rare memorabilia worth more than my entire house. Harris, who knows a quail-hunting friend of

Tom Huggler and Fagin
by Jim Foote

Plate III

mine from Georgia, is the perfect host, and six of us enjoy a succulent dinner of roasted ring-necked duck with wild rice and onion pie.

After dinner Frank makes Bogsuckers—four parts gin and one part dry sherry, garnished with olives skewered on a black locust thorn with a woodcock feather at one end. Harris tells me how much he enjoys hunting woodcock in the floodlands when the morning duck flights have slowed. I insist on only one Bogsucker when Frank attempts to refill my glass. Later that night I will dream of being chased by a twenty-foot-long alligator and wonder if the nightmare is prompted by the drink or the pictures of monstrous gators on the lodge walls.

The talk drifts to woodcock guns and Harris excuses himself a moment, then returns with a .410 high-grade Parker, one of three Parkers he owns (his late father passed down the other two). The .410 was made to Frank's specifications with original engraving by Robert Runge, who began working on Parker upgrades in 1933 and is still at it in his eighties. The gold inlays show a woodcock and a likeness of Frank's now-gone Brittany, Topper, a dog I would have loved to hunt behind. One-of-a-kind guns like this are difficult to appraise but are considered nearly priceless. I wince when Charley snaps shut the breech, then swings through an imaginary bird. You should close a gun like that as carefully as you would the clasp on an empress' diamond necklace.

A Fall of Woodcock

I offer Frank a signed copy of a book I wrote about grouse and note a little moisture gather in his eyes. It is a memorable evening and a fitting close to my Bayou State adventure. I laugh as hard as anyone when the subject turns to writing about my experiences. Larry, one of Harris' friends and hunting partners, looks at me through his raised glass, which has the effect of magnifying his eye to huge proportion.

"Yankee woodcock hunters are like hemorrhoids," Larry says. "You are welcome to come down so long as you don't stay. And you have to remember to go back up."

Later, I wonder if I should have given Larry a book, too.

8

MICHIGAN AND THE GREAT LAKES

I let a woodcock go last fall, and I'm not sure why I didn't *poof* the twittering target with a load of 9s just as the bird hesitated at the canopy of poplar whips.

Was the shot too easy? Am I getting soft?

I don't know, because I fired at the next three woodcock that leaped above the understory of bracken fern as though the birds had strapped air lifts to their feet. Two of those woodcock found their way into the game pouch, then onto my dinner plate that evening. So why did I allow the earlier bird, perhaps a migrating female, to whiffle up and away to safety without my firing as much as a salutation?

A Fall of Woodcock

Maybe it was because the bird and my setter shared a five-minute trance that had nothing to do with me. Perhaps it was the fragile October light, offering illumination to subdued reds, yellows, and browns (must we *always* shatter such tranquility?). Consider the bird itself, whose bright eye bore at me as it stitched its way skyward. Woodcock are the absolute essence of autumn; mysteriously they arrive in a whisper amidst swirls of beige and brown.

I cannot imagine hunting across autumn without the prospect of seeing woodcock. It would be worse than going to the duck blind and never getting to watch a greenhead mallard, wings cupped, brake to the decoys. Worse than spending a month bowhunting from a tree stand and never spotting a deer sneak by below. Oddly enough, when I participate in those and other fall sports, it is my favorite game bird, the woodcock, that I often think about.

I am a lucky man to live in Michigan, which typically leads the nation in the annual number of woodcock harvested although that fact occurs simply because more hunters seek woodcock here than anywhere else. In 1990 Michigan produced a quarter-million birds for about 75,000 hunters. By comparison, Wisconsin yielded 140,000 woodcock for 37,000 hunters, and Minnesota gave up 114,000 birds to 27,000 hunters. The only other state with a harvest exceeding 100,000 that year was Louisiana (143,000 woodcock for 21,000 hunters).

MICHIGAN AND THE GREAT LAKES

These numbers can fluctuate greatly from year to year. In 1993 only 17,000 Minnesota hunters took to the woods to kill 68,000 woodcock for an average of four birds each. Some 34,700 Wisconsin hunters spent 213,000 days afield to take 118,000 woodcock for an average of 3.4 birds each. In Michigan 67,380 hunters spent 956,430 days bagging 194,130 birds. At only 2.88 birds each, their average take was the lowest of the region.

Here, in the Great Lakes region, the number of hunters depends on whether grouse populations

A Fall of Woodcock

are cycling high or low. Again, forest gamebird hunters typically seek grouse, and consider woodcock a bonus bird, although this attitude is changing. In Louisiana, weather appears to be the biggest factor that drives the number of hunters and the number of woodcock they kill. Five years earlier, three times that number of hunters shot three times as many woodcock.

In Minnesota the season opens September 1; in Wisconsin and Michigan, the openers occur in mid-September. I can't be serious about the sport in September when coverts are too thick, temperatures too warm, and birds too scattered or in small family pods. I don't like to shoot at woodcock when all I can see is a wing flashing through the undergrowth, when mosquitoes drill through the sweat beads on my forehead.

During the Great Lakes seasons' waning days of November, most of the migrants have passed on, and only a few straggling males remain. They move with the frost line: southern Michigan, central Illinois, northern Missouri. That leaves October as the right time to hunt woodcock in the Great Lakes states. October and woodcock are forever fused in my mind.

Woodcock sometimes find their way west of the Mississippi River, even though they are largely eastern game birds. Some of those reared in the Maritime Provinces and New England move on through the Middle Atlantic states to winter in the

Michigan and the Great Lakes

Carolinas, Georgia, and the Florida panhandle. The migration is not so much a solid push of birds as it is a trickle, and it is not always due south, according to the birds' mental compasses. Prevailing wind, temperatures, and the abundance or scarcity of earthworms cause a considerable amount of east and west drifting. Most East Coast birds, for example, follow the spine of the Appalachians into West Virginia and Tennessee. Sometimes they link up with Midwest birds wandering down the Ohio and Mississippi rivers to end up in Alabama, Mississippi, and most important, Louisiana, where experts estimate that upwards of 70 percent of the continental population spends the winter.

Each October my own annual migrations take me throughout Michigan and on into Wisconsin and Minnesota. Years of record keeping in my home state have told me that the first two weeks of October is the best time to hunt in the Upper Peninsula. The middle two weeks of the month find migrants pushing through the northern half of the lower peninsula. Friends tell me the same pattern occurs in Wisconsin and Minnesota, and I have experienced it to some degree but not enough to be personally convinced it is fact. As October wanes, woodcock wax strong in the southern regions of all three states. Certain coverts I have gunned for years near my downstate Michigan home almost always hold woodcock the week before Halloween. Most years by Veterans Day I can't find a bird there on a bet.

A Fall of Woodcock

Harvest records kept by the Michigan Department of Natural Resources (DNR) show that during a recent year, the top three counties were Chippewa, Oceania, and Muskegon. Chippewa is in the U.P., Oceania and Muskegon are in the middle of the lower peninsula. The point is that woodcock traverse the entire state, as well as most of Wisconsin and Minnesota. For this reason, the number of birds available in any given year will not affect when and where I seek them. I simply consider the calendar and go where I expect them to be.

Looking over field notes for a recent autumn, I see that friends and I flushed twenty-five birds on September 30, forty-seven on October 1, and thirty-one on October 2 from western Upper Peninsula counties that border Wisconsin. In Osceola County (northern lower Michigan), I flushed twelve woodcock during a short hunt on October 12 and a memorable forty birds farther south in Mason County on October 22. Three days later in southern Michigan's Tuscola County, a friend and I moved twenty woodcock in only two hours.

So the date-book is the place to start, but it is always wise to consult the weather gods, too. For years I traveled to the eastern Upper Peninsula, and although I usually managed to see a few woodcock, along with grouse, I rarely hit it just right—when birds were skulking under every bush. Then one fall I began watching daily weather reports with care and keeping in touch with local DNR field office personnel every couple of days to keep on top of conditions.

On the morning of October 9, I received the weather report I wanted: "Clear skies, freezing temperatures, northwest winds gusting to 20 mph predicted for tonight." I loaded my dogs and aimed the pickup north. Along the way I stopped at the Music Box (every serious woodcock hunter has pet names for pet coverts—show me yours, I may show you mine), which is a roadside patch of aspen fringed with alders that had provided a dozen flushes the weekend before. I assumed those were local birds. Today, though, the cupboard was empty.

One hundred thirty miles north of the Music Box, I crossed the Mackinac Bridge while a light snow speckled the windshield. Now in the U.P., I set up a tent in a state-forest campground, then went to sleep to the sound of a flapping rain fly. Next morning I awoke to a bottomless blue sky and discovered that the dogs' water bowls supported a skim of ice—perfect woodcock hunting conditions.

The place I had in mind was a tangle of aspen with an understory of red osier dogwood and the odd juniper. I called it The Farm Belt. To the north lay a half-mile of pasture ground studded with boulders and beyond the pasture, a river. This was dairy farm country, and I figured the woodcock—whether they were from Michigan or Ontario or both places—would move with the favorable wind along the river from forests to the north and west, then pile into the

A Fall of Woodcock

first decent habitat they could find. I was not disappointed. Although I shot poorly that day, my setter, Macbeth, in her first serious effort at woodcocking, pinned thirty-five birds.

The next day the Music Box was stiff with woodcock.

Time and again, over some three decades now, I have used the calendar to plan my hunting forays. Many years ago, when I used to teach in a southern Michigan high school, I chanced upon a small drop of flight woodock in an alder spit a few miles from the school. The date was October 23. The next year the birds showed up on October 25 and the year after that on October 19. I doubt if they were the same woodcock, and yet I could make book that every fall between October 19 and 30, that two-acre boggy patch of alders would host a small band of birds.

How do I know they were flight woodcock and not local birds? I didn't. The only clue is to be lucky enough to shoot a banded bird and then find out where it was reared. Arming yourself with that information won't prove that the other birds you shoot that day were reared in the same place as the banded one. A thick layer of body fat along a woodcock's breast and thighs is simply evidence that the bird is healthy and capable of sustained flight. It does not prove the woodcock is on the migratory move.

When I flush ten woodcock in any given covert, I begin to think they are probably flight birds.

When the rate goes to ten flushes per hour, I'm quite certain of it. But I'm never positive.

We think of woodcock as north-to-south migrants, but the truth is they drift to all points of the compass although the overall movement is definitely to the south. I have found them along sand-soiled, sumac-covered hillsides a mile or more from water, and I have flushed and shot them from standing fields of corn, in sprawling fields of goldenrod and other weeds, and once in a trashy soybean field. In northern Michigan where friends and I go in early October, we typically locate birds in young aspen slashings from two to twelve years old. Dry weather sends them—and us—to alders and other lowland cover sprinkled with, but not dominated by, evergreen habitat.

On days of pelting rain we often flush woodcock loitering under juniper spreads, little thickets of hemlock, or individual balsam fir trees where they wait out the deluge. During wet falls, I have jumped woodcock from dry hummocks of drowned red osier dogwood and even flooded timber where they sometimes share daytime loafing habitat with snipe.

I distinctly remember one fall when a favorite covert of birches mixed with alders and witch hazel was flooded from heavy rains. Donning knee-high rubber boots, I slipped in behind my white dog, who splashed on ahead. Macbeth's bell suddenly stopped, and I had to look hard to find her among several wind-fallen birches. The bird we sent aloft was faster and smaller than a woodcock. I knew it was a snipe as I pulled the trigger; my dog confirmed the fact with a soggy retrieve. The next bird up was a woodcock, and the one after that, a snipe again. The birds were hiding in dry pockets of ground cover. Of the dozen we flushed, half were snipe and half were woodcock.

More than 60 percent of Michigan's annual harvest of woodcock occurs in the northern half of the lower peninsula, a reflection of both hunter density and young-growth habitat. Upper Peninsula and southern Michigan hunters share equally the remainder. In Minnesota, woodcock are found primarily in forested areas of the central and northcentral region where aspen is plentiful and lots of public land assure access. Key counties are Itasca, Aitkin, Koochiching, Cass, and southern St. Louis. Although gunning for flight birds occurs in southern farmland woodlots, the land is mostly private and access is difficult. The top Wisconsin counties in a recent year were Forest, Langlade, and Oneida—all located in the northeast region. The northcentral region is also good, but birds fly throughout the state, and many on private land never encounter hunters.

Hunters in other Midwest states can determine similar timetables for flight woodcock. For example, a friend of mine from northern Missouri, where the hunting season typically lasts until mid-December, intercepts birds within a week either side of Halloween. Another friend, from Iowa, seeks willow coverts along eastern rivers that drain into the Mississippi. His best hunting occurs from mid-October to late November. During mild winters some woodcock may not migrate farther south than these states and eastern Kansas.

Wherever you hunt them in the northcentral region (by this I mean the Great Lakes states and those of the upper midwest—namely Ohio, Illinois, and Indiana), certain common denominators come into play. Bear in mind that woodcock move through a succession of habitat types as Indian summer gives way to full-blown fall. Early on, the birds hole up in aspen whips, especially along those fringed with alder. If you lose your hat every now and then, the habitat is probably thick enough. As the leaves start to drop, woodcock move to stands of ten- to twenty-foot-high aspens (aka poplars). About the time the unclothed uplands begin to freeze, the birds will shift into mixed hardwoods and conifers. As the weather grows colder, they spend their final north-country days along last-to-freeze creek bottoms and cloaking evergreens.

As I learned in Louisiana, migrants seek coverts similar in structure to the final northern stage. Though the actual vegetation may change as they venture south, they want similar leafy canopies to twenty feet tall; moist, thickly brushed streams; and old fields and orchards returning to woody cover. As the coverts grow gaunt from leaf drop, understories figure more importantly. Typical understories include dogwood and witch hazel, frost-killed bracken fern that is brown and flagging, blackberry canes and other briers. Ground cover is usually scant.

Strange weather patterns can alter these rules, and seasonal shifts in climate may void them altogether. During the drought years of 1988 and 1989, I shot few woodcock in my favorite coverts of upland aspen because the birds exclusively favored lowland alders. But oddities occur all the time. For example, because woodcock in the western U.P. are mostly all reared locally, you would expect coverts to be bare once the birds move on. But a Baraga County hunter I know gets top gunning during the first week of November, even when the ground has turned to iron in some places. On November 5, 6, and 7 of a recent year, he flushed seventy-one, fifty-four and forty-one woodcock respectively. His best day afield, prior to that trifecta, produced only eleven flushes. Where did that major drop of woodcock come from? No one knows.

How far do woodcock migrate during any given night? Greg Sepik told me about a Maine bird that had been fitted with radio telemetry at Moosehorn National Wildlife Refuge. Researchers last monitored the woodcock during the day of November 7. A major migration occurred that night, and after sunset the bird was heard no more. Two days later a hunter shot it near Hyde Park, New York, 450 miles away.

Michigan and the Great Lakes

A Fall of Woodcock

Another consideration: Woodcock and ruffed grouse don't share the same primary habitats although the two species do overlap each other's preferences. In general, grouse like bigger timber, but the truth is I find more grouse in "woodcock" habitat (wrist-thick aspens) than the reverse.

When poplar is cut, it regenerates immediately, sending suckers of new growth to explode above the ground. At only two or three years old, these stands—called whips or slashings—may attract and hold woodcock, especially early in the season. Some of the best sport I know occurs in aspen whips that are only neck-high because you have the luxury of seeing your birds for clear shots and pinpoint marks. In the Great Lakes region, renewed interest in timber cutting by huge companies like Mead, Louisiana Pacific, and Champion is producing good woodcock habitat.

Upper Peninsula clearcuts in particular may be miles long, however, and it is easy to get turned around in them. A couple of years ago, a veteran hunter in his late seventies lost himself in an enormous clearcut where I have also hunted. Instead of panicking when darkness arrived, the old timer curled up on the ground between his two Belton setters and slept as well as possible. The next day searchers found him (Blaze Orange and white dogs helped), suffering from a mild case of dehydration. Next year he was back in the same covert (this time with a compass in his pocket).

Forest fires help create openings for singing males to set up new territories. The growth of ground cover and regeneration of young forest produces brood and rearing habitat. I think of the Tower Burn near Ely, Minnesota. In May of 1992 some seven thousand acres burned in this excellent grouse and woodcock hunting region at the base of the Boundary Waters Canoe Area. The burn encompassed a mixture of forestland owned by St. Louis County, the state of Minnesota, and the Potlatch Corporation. It is all open to hunting.

I have learned that woodcock use niches within such sprawling coverts. Rarely are they spread throughout. You might walk for hours, stumbling over tops and drops and cursing the loggers who windrowed them that way to make your personal obstacle course, without moving a bird. Then, suddenly, your dog may stick four or five in a row. A fellow I know from Vermont once came to Michigan in October and never fired a shell at woodcock although he did manage to pot a few grouse. Used to hunting small coverts of abandoned apple orchards and streamside groves at home, he was intimidated by mile-wide clearcuts and avoided them altogether. What a shame.

Macbeth's bell has quit, or so I think. After all, it is hard to hear a tinkle above the whine of southbound, Sunday-afternoon traffic on nearby I-75 north of Grayling, Michigan. I had last spotted her moments ago in a thick poplar slashing ahead and to

A Fall of Woodcock

the left. Circling a small wet spot, I step into the bamboo. There she is, stone still except for her wrinkling lip. In slow motion, Macbeth's eyes look from me to the leaf-littered ground before her. Hers are the eyes of November, fervent and brown, and they are talking to me.

Yo, Tom. Right under my nose. See 'em?

Of course, I cannot.

We bird hunters live for tension like that. As a child, I remember not wanting to rip open a Christmas present that looked suspiciously like a .22 Hornet. I felt it for a long time before carefully removing the wrapping. I was the kind of anal-retentive kid who saved the cake frosting for last, if you know what I mean. Years later, in a San Francisco restaurant, I unnerved the Japanese chef who prepared a sumptuous meal before us by eating it in slow motion. He mistakenly thought I wasn't pleased.

Waiting for a six-ounce bird to explode from cover, then whisk itself away in jinking flight, is a little like those experiences.

Now, neither I nor Macbeth could stand the pressure any longer. I stepped into the space between us, and a tawny-colored bird tacked up and away on soft, fluttering wings. I caught the woodcock at the roof of leaves with a load of No. 8 shot, and she floated to earth as in a dream. A couple hundred yards away, the traffic moved along, oblivious to such high drama.

I was here by design. If woodcock follow rivers, why don't they follow roads? To a woodcock on the move at dusk or during the night, I believe that roadways—especially those that are paved—may well look like rivers. The bird's rapid-fire metabolism and the demands of long flight mean it must eat often and well. Rivers and roads eventually lead to moist-earth areas where worms are abundant. Some of the best roadside coverts where I have found woodcock over the years are miles from the nearest river. The first few times this oddity occurred, I shrugged it off to coincidence. Now, I believe they occur by design—woodcock use certain thoroughfares as deliberate travel corridors.

One of my favorite coverts is The Church, a ten-acre triangle of young-growth aspen along a major highway in northern lower Michigan. The east- and west-running highway is cut by two county gravel roads. One road comes in from the west and bends due south. The other crosses the highway about a quarter-mile east of the first county road, then jogs southwest to join the first. The result is a triangle shape, with the apex at its western end. Incoming woodcock hit this point of cover, find it to their liking, and drop in throughout its length. On a good day, I can take a five-bird limit—though I stop at three these days—within one hundred fifty yards of my truck.

I have also been skunked here. As any woodcock hunter knows, these mercurial birds can be as

A Fall of Woodcock

unreliable as a pocket watch stuck to a magnet. Still, certain conditions at least offer the potential for good roadside hunting (individual state laws may prohibit hunting on or near roads—check the regulations first). Consider the wind factor. Will woodcock fly into the teeth of a twenty-knot wind? They can, but I doubt if they will. Instead, they'll wait for a tailwind, especially if they have plenty to eat and are in no hurry.

Steve Smith, a friend of mine, did a master's degree research project on how woodcock use topography and weather when migrating. He learned that woodcock travel on tailwinds along river valleys, especially on starlit nights. On nights with cloud cover or no wind, the birds are likely to stay put or, at best, move only a short distance to better worming grounds. They often follow east- or west-flowing streams to where they join south-running rivers. There they pile up until the wind is right and/or cold, clear nights tighten their banquet table and shut off the food supply.

One of the fastest hunts I ever participated in occurred years ago in northern lower Michigan's Montmorency County. The covert was a fifteen-acre swath of chest-high, three-year-old aspen, which now holds grouse but no woodcock. This particular honey hole is on the east side of a north-south, two-lane highway. Two partners and I tackled it one afternoon late in October when the covert was growing gaunt. It was raining—a condition, I learned long ago, that can make for good gunning because woodcock

Michigan and the Great Lakes

A Fall of Woodcock

hold more tightly (they don't want to get wet any more than hunters do). A flight must have touched down during the night because our nose-sticking dogs went a tad crazy over all the scent. Points were often mere yards apart. In all, we flushed twenty-eight woodcock.

Surely you have heard stories of migrant woodcock skimming over rivers at dusk like flocks of teal. I've never seen it myself—that is, no more than three or four birds in the air at once. But a bowhunting friend of mine sat in his deer blind in northern Michigan one evening last October and counted more than one hundred woodcock drift through, mostly in singles and pairs, sometimes in bunches up to six birds. At dark he walked back to his car and drove home along the same highway the woodcock had paralleled.

In a recent year 4 million drivers crossed the Mackinac Bridge into Michigan's Upper Peninsula. Most were tourists seeking solitude and natural beauty among the one hundred fifty waterfalls and seventeen hundred miles of Lake Superior and Lake Michigan shoreline the U.P. offers. Many were fishermen who came to sample the region's four thousand inland lakes and twelve thousand miles of streams, and some were hunters seeking big game, grouse, and woodcock. Ninety percent of the U.P. is forested, and some half of its 11 million acres (more land than the three southern New England states, combined with Delaware) is open to public hunting.

Nearly one third of Michigan's land mass lies above the Straits of Mackinac, and yet only 3½ percent of all Michiganders live there. At 384 miles wide, the U.P.'s western extremity at Ironwood is farther west than St. Louis. Copper Harbor, on the tip of the Keweenaw Peninsula, which juts into Lake Superior like a little finger, is farther north than Montreal. The U.P. is home to only eighteen people per square mile, but no one lives farther than thirty miles from a shopping mall.

Those facts say nothing about the U.P. mystique. This is the land Hemingway idealized through Nick Adams, the place where Judge John Voelker (aka Robert Traver) fished brook trout and wrote *Anatomy of a Murder* and *Trout Magic*. The discovery of iron ore in 1844 at Negaunee was more important to America's economic and industrial development than the California gold rush of the same era. The U.P. has long been a place for discovery and adventure. As such, it has attracted copper miners from Cornwall, timber cutters from Finland, trout fishermen from Peoria, and woodcock and grouse hunters from everywhere.

The residents, many of whom call themselves Yoopers, are as open or closed as anywhere else, I suppose. One time I lost the key to the double locks on my dog trailer. It was growing dark and there was

A Fall of Woodcock

no place open where I could borrow a bolt cutter. In desperation I knocked on the door of a small house tucked away along a county road near Engadine. The name of the man who answered was Lawrence Vallier, and he used an acetylene torch to cut free the locks after I backed the trailer into his workshop. Lawrence wouldn't take a dime but did gratefully accept a grouse and brace of woodcock, which I cleaned for him in his back yard while he held the flashlight.

Another time, a burly man threatened me in a Crystal Falls bar because I was one of those "damn downstate" writers who sent too many deer hunters to the U.P. Certain loggers can be bad medicine, too. Jouncing in my pickup along a two-track near Amasa one morning, I narrowly missed being run down by an immense logging truck bearing a thirty-ton load of pulp and careening along at forty miles an hour. Just before I dived for the undergrowth, I saw the driver flip me the bird. No, you don't have to go to the U.P. to meet all kinds of people. There just may be a few more fringe types living there.

At a McDonald's restaurant in Marquette in the westcentral Upper Peninsula, I stand in line ahead of a family that looks like tough times are at hand. Father, a thin man with square glasses and brown polyester pants too short for his spider legs, wonders about my motorhome parked outside: "Do I like it?

How's the gas mileage?" I can hardly get in my order for his machine-gun questions.

I take an empty booth, and he herds his family into the next one, also vacant. He sits closest to me and next to Mother, a pleasant but plain woman in a long drab skirt, whose hair is drawn severely into an unattractive bun. I wonder if they are Mennonite. More questions. "Wouldn't a travel trailer make more sense? Have I ever pulled a travel trailer? What do I think of them?" The answers, delivered between bites of my Big Mac, only spawn more questions.

"What's in the trailer? What's the difference between a setter and a Brittany?" Mother and their children, a boy and girl in their early teens I assume, eat their Quarter-Pounders and fries in silence. Periodically, the kids steal shy glances my way, then look at each other in the collegial way of study-hall gossips.

Father sips on his black coffee—he's ordered nothing to eat for himself—and ponders the next round of interrogation. It seems he wants to travel with his family, and he's in the market for an RV of some sort. "What do they cost?" he wonders.

I tell him the motorhome is worth about fifty thousand, and he swallows hard what, I guess, is scalding coffee. I hand him my napkin.

The man coughs, then resumes his questions. When they begin to repeat themselves, I have a creeping suspicion that he may have a diagnosis. Or a hearing problem. His wife smiles when I look at her, a trace of pleading on my face. She gets up and brings me some napkins so I can finish my meal.

"We came up here on our honeymoon from Milwaukee," her husband is saying, "and we've been trying to figure out how to get back ever since."

I suggest he rent a small travel trailer to see if RVing fits his lifestyle. "Do you camp?" I ask.

"No. We sold our tent in a yard sale. We live in the woods now. I cut a little pulp."

Trying to expand the conversation, I ask what grade the kids are in. More secret smiles.

"They're home-schooled," Mother says, pleasantly.

"So they get all As?" I quip.

Father shifts uncomfortably in his seat, the dialogue moving dangerously out of orbit now. "What do you hunt with those dogs out there in your trailer?" he makes a valiant effort to bring it back.

"Woodcock. And grouse. Got any back there in the woods where you live?"

"Well, we have to go now," he announces, jumping up and slipping a leather cap over his graying hair. The children gather their remaining fries and do not look up again. Mother purses her lips in a faint smile. He shakes my hand. His hand feels like that of a laborer—sandpaper, the coarse stuff.

I don't like fast food. It is tasteless and expensive. I eat it for convenience and so I grow annoyed, fingers drumming on the truck dash, if the wait is more than a few minutes. I like unpretentious, out-of-the-way places where the food is homemade and served on time. The best meals in England are the simple, unadorned fare served with pints of beer or ale at neighborhood pubs, and the same can be said for northern Michigan taverns. Ma Deeter's in Luzerne and the Owl Cafe in Alpena come to mind. You can get a bowl of good chili at the Hungry Tummy in Beulah, a twenty-ounce T-bone at the Antlers in Sault Ste. Marie, and cabbage-sized cinnamon rolls at the Poor Boy in McMillan. The Gallery in St. Ignace has fried whitefish livers if you like that sort of thing (I do). Want great pizza? Try the little bar in Ralph, where deer hunters have papered the ceiling with dollar bills. A fine burger? The hotel bar in Amasa.

  I shed a hungry tear when the Trading Post, a converted logging camp dating to 1923, finally limped out of business. Over a Lumberjack Sandwich for $2.25 and a thirty-two-ounce draft for the same price (no wonder owners Bill and Marge Borland from suburban Detroit went broke), I liked to replay the day's events in bird coverts while listening to "The Wreck of the Edmund Fitzgerald" on the 1941 Wurlitzer nickelodeon that Borland had found in a back room and converted from 32 volts to 110.

A Fall of Woodcock

It's an old story: When a great place goes down, you miss it terribly, but then another steps in to take its place. If you hunt birds, you find them.

On a warm afternoon in early October, a friend and I stop at the bar in Randville, which also goes by the name of Harworth, on M-95 north of Iron Mountain. We are thirsty and tired and have left open the truck tailgate so the dogs can get some relief. "Good hayin' weather," says a red-faced young farmer, climbing down from his Farmall M, which he leaves running in the tavern parking lot. He clears his throat in anticipation of the cold beer a few steps away. "Good weather, all right, 'cept our crop is one-third of normal."

"Supposed to rain tonight," I answer. "Then snow."

"That's why I'm cutting today."

Inside, nearly every kind of bird and game animal native to the Great Lakes region is represented along the knotty-pine walls. The lacquer is a dull orange from years of tobacco smoke. Raccoons, foxes, deer and bear, a woodcock with bulging eyes, a day-old fawn, and several small grouse are all dark and discolored with age. So are a six-foot-long alligator and pair of Arctic owls.

"Every one was donated," smiles Dottie Sayler, who lives in Aura and who recently bought the bar along with some hundred years of history. "And every one has a story."

Michigan and the Great Lakes

The story I'd like to hear is about the buck with baggy face made of leather. According to a sign hanging from its neck, an Indian hand-crafted the "work of art" in 1890. He must have been drunk.

At a corner table pulp cutters still wearing their yellow hard hats are drinking bottled beer. I wonder if they work for Louisiana Pacific, which recently opened a new mill just up the road. I'm tempted to ask them the whereabouts of cuttings but decide to wait awhile.

The enormous bar is made of polished mahogany and a brass foot rail runs its length. Behind the counter is a proud mahogany cabinet with glass windows and the name "Minwegan and Weiss." I'm sure it's worth plenty. A full-mount, twelve-point buck stands just off the side entrance. A metal locking tag suggests the deer was shot in 1953, but it could just as easily have been poached.

My partner and I order beef-and-cheese sandwiches, the ingredients for which Dottie slices on a 1912 Hobart cutter. Blind robins roost on a card next to the Green Bay Packers schedule and a jar of nasty-looking pork hocks. The television above the bar is thankfully silent. Outside, the Oregon, California, and Eastern locomotive woofs, and its whistle hangs low and reverberates in the humidity. The hard hats don't bother to look up. Two ceiling fans whir away, and no one has the energy to rack the pool balls.

The farmer, sitting next to us, drains his longneck and orders another.

A Fall of Woodcock

"What are you hunting with them dogs?" he asks. "Birds?"

"That's it," I assure him. "Grouse and woodcock."

"Woodcock?" one of the loggers suddenly cuts in. "Is that them little birds with the long bill? We saw a bunch this morning on our way into the Michigamme Tract, didn't we, Pete?"

My entree has arrived.

A fall of woodcock into a covert you have either chosen or to which you have been directed, is a magic all its own. You did not see the birds arrive in the abyss of night, of course, but they are there. You know it when your little Brittany, Max, smashing through the boot tangle to retrieve the morning's first kill, jams the brakes and whirls into a second point—his bratwurst tail quivering with anticipation. It does not matter if you kill this second bird because soon another will flush and another after that.

You and Max move through the covert with the efficiency of an NBA full-court press, trapping woodcock and toeing them aloft. An hour later, the game is over, and the woodcock have won: twenty-two flushes, only two birds in your game bag for ten shots.

It is October and the ghosts of the Druids are stirring. The bewitching hour you just experienced stars *ignis fatuus*, the will-o'-the-wisp that comes and goes with the mysteriousness of the full moon. The magic of flight woodcock occurs throughout eastern North America but is best enjoyed in the second-growth forests of Minnesota, Wisconsin and Michigan. These are the prime breeding grounds for our little poltergeist with the ice-pick bill.

9

BIRD CAMP

Bad weather hit bird camp early that year. Every couple of hours it seemed as though someone wrung the sodden gray blanket that shrouded Michigan's Upper Peninsula from DeTour Village to Ironwood, and we hunted between downpours. The trunks of the maples shone black like wet Angus steers; the leafy crowns smoldered yellow with surrealistic fire. We were coming down out of the aspen uplands, my truck lurching in the flooded ruts of the two-track, headlights wobbling into the cold, darkening woods.

I stopped when the low beams caught a woodcock in the trail. We watched for a long moment, wipers swishing away the spattering snow and slanting across the bird who eyed us in turn. Then, a rush of apricot and he was gone into the night. I drove on, the warm pickup smelling of October with its leaf mold and dog hair, wet clothing and subdued anticipation.

We were chilled and tired and hungry. Breakfast, days ago it seemed, was scant enough—coffee and a roll. Then someone had forgotten the sandwiches and so, in the woods, thirty miles from town, we pooled what we could find for lunch. A jug of cider, loaf of bread, and a half-stick of venison sausage disappear quickly when rationed among eight men. Now, we wanted drinks and steaks and a hot motel shower. A warm bed would be nice. We drove past a dozen places, all lit up in tempting neon. Had we yielded, I would not be telling this story in the same way.

We were headed for Bird Camp, our Spartan digs in a state forest campground an hour's drive away. When we pulled in off the highway, maple leaves sticking to our tires, the camp was without life, without cheer. I had the feeling I had made a terrible mistake. From the back seat, Steve must have read my mind: "Forget the sandwiches in that cooler," he said. "We're going to have a meal no one will ever forget."

Slowly, the lanterns sputtered and bathed the scene in yellow light. Those of us with dogs toweled and fed them. Two of my friends set about cleaning birds while another raided his cache of dry wood and

Bird Camp

got a fire started. There is nothing like a campfire to drive back the night, lift the spirit. A bottle of home brew, malty and dark, helps. About the time the beer was gone, Steve, who maintains a tremendous vegetable garden at home, had put together a fresh, wonderful salad with Swiss chard, endives, and Roma tomatoes.

The next course was broiled woodcock breasts. They had been marinating all day in a rich stew of Worcestershire sauce, fresh-crushed garlic, and olive oil. Wrapping a piece of bacon around each, I skewered the bacon with a toothpick, arranged the offering on the grill, and broiled for a minute on each side. If you like your beefsteak rare, like I do, you must eat woodcock the same way. Every bite, and there aren't many, is like a taste of the best filet mignon. Overcook the meat, even a bit, and it will be unpalatable.

While I was tending to the woodcock, Steve fired up his Durango, a heavy-duty, LP-fueled grill that is the ultimate for outdoor cooking (I'm told the company is out of business—if you find a Durango in a garage sale, buy it without regard to cost). Soon, the sharp odor and wild sizzle of Cajun-blackened lake trout permeated the air. Someone broke out a jug of cheap Chardonnay, just right for lancing the heat of cayenne pepper.

Imagine a circle of grown men, some still standing, others balancing paper plates on knees, their happy, boyish faces awash with yellow-and-red camp-fire light. Courses of venison ratatouille, of grouse tarragon with heavy cream, and the grand finale of cherries jubilee—each round appearing as though by magic from a slap-together kitchen with no running water, arranged through an act of love by a gourmand who clenches a flashlight in his teeth.

Now, picture the embers burning low, the storyteller's voice lulled with brandy, the soft cough from cigar smoke reminding him he has late-hour listeners. It is nearly midnight and the clouds have parted to allow a glimpse of the half-moon. The storyteller pauses, and we listen for another sound. There it is again, the croaking call from somewhere high above. A flock of sandhills, lifted from the Oligocene

Bird Camp

for this night's curtain call, are pinwheeling their steady way south. We lift glasses in thanks.

Every October, when the blood quickens and the hardwoods burn with silent fires of red, orange, yellow and gold, we leave our wives for four days. Bird Camp is a Big Tingle for each of us, and it is all perfectly legal.

It started innocently enough when I invited Norris to join me in the Upper Peninsula one fall about fifteen years ago. We had a swell time, hunting new coverts, many of which held birds, and tenting under the stars in a primitive campground. The DNR calls these six-dollars-a-night campgrounds "rustic." Translation: hand-pumped water so cold your wrists ache, vault toilets without seats or paper, rickety picnic tables with no space for new graffiti, and no people (the best part). Next year Norris invited a pal and so did I. The group grew. When it reached ten men, we decided to hold it right there. A decade later no one has dropped out to make room for the Middle Eastern chef from Chicago I've had my eye on. And we hope no one does quit, because a noticeable void occurs when anyone skips a year.

It happened to Jerry one fall when family illness kept him home, to Steve the time he lost his job, and to Norris, fresh from the surgeon's scalpel. Dave and I have been caught in various editorial fires and have had to cancel, he one year, me the next. But we're a brutal bunch. The year I scratched, they sent me a camp photo where every mother's son is vigorously giving me the finger. I might as well have gone because I missed my magazine deadline anyway. My mind was on Bird Camp the whole time it went on without me.

I knew, for example, that at five o'clock on Wednesday Tom was pouring snoots of blackberry brandy into nine Dixie cups, our equivalent to lighting the Olympic flame. I wondered if Randy, who never has to help erect the carnival-sized cook tent because he drives all night from Flint where, unlike most of us, he has a day job, made it up safely without creaming a deer with his big GMC van; or, if he did hit a deer, if he'd remember to salvage the backstraps for hors d'oeuvres. Every night around dinner time, I wondered what poacher's tale Jim, our resident state conservation officer, was telling, and whether his spicy baked bean ragu would have the same hand-grenade effect the next day; what disgusting limerick Tom was reciting; what tasteless Hoosier joke Ron, his brown eyes dilated behind his glasses, was relating.

The late John Voelker once signed a script of paper declaring Norris the U.P. Cribbage Champ. Who dares take on the champ tonight? Were Dick's bluegills as tasty this year as last? Did Jerry make it to the sleeping bag, or sleep outside on the ground, again, in his red-and-black plaid Mackinaw? I wondered if Dave shot another snowshoe hare and if Steve roped it to Dave's pickup or cleaned the hare

Bird Camp

and sent it into the marinating pot? And what about the woodcock? Are the boys finding enough birds to take some home this year, and are they making the dogs proud?

I'll never miss Bird Camp again.

I hunted alone that day in the cold drizzle, and when I got back to camp about noon, the place was deserted, the boys all out hunting. They wouldn't be back until dark, perhaps earlier if the rain changed to snow, maybe later if they holed up somewhere to watch the Michigan–Michigan State game. It didn't matter. I had all afternoon to fix the evening meal, our last one of the year.

You knew the end was near because the place was a mess. Unwashed cooking pots and frying pans roosted atop the picnic tables inside the U.S. Army squad tent we used as a mess hall. The closest trash containers fairly groaned, their lids askew atop bulging contents. We've had raccoons invade camp in the past—including one bold devil that tipped over an uncorked fifteen-dollar bottle of extra-virgin olive oil—but, luckily, no bears. A habituated bear could do a lot of damage while eating his way to Nirvana, maybe even forcing a grocery run to Escanaba. Our food bill is already high enough. One year it ran four-hundred and fifty bucks, for only eight guys. And that didn't include the party-store incidentals.

But that was the year we had étouffée, made with fresh shrimp flown in from New Orleans. The étouffée was Norris' idea. On the last day of camp the year before, we were having our parting meeting, nine grown men hunkering around a dying campfire as serious as though we were planning the liberation of Kuwait, which, incidentally was where Larry had gone on a government contract to defuse land mines. "What would you like to eat next year?" asked Steve, our self-schooled chef. Steve used to plan all the meals and do nearly all the cooking but didn't get to hunt much. You can't prepare dishes like Lamb Souvlaki or Marsala Chicken and also have time to get lost in the woods. Now we all help plan and prepare, which was why I was back in camp early today. Out of nowhere Norris said, "How about Shrimp Étouffée? You made a helluva bouillabaisse the other night. Bet your étouffée makes men leave home."

  Remembering these details made me laugh while I washed dishes and tidied up the camp. Then I dumped a bag of briquettes in the Weber grill, arranged them around an empty coffee can, doused the charcoal with lighter fluid, and set it afire. Next I retrieved a venison hind quarter from the massive marine cooler I had brought and went to work. One of my favorite recipes, Grilled Venison Roast, is easy to prepare. Boning out the entire haunch and trimming away all membranes and fat create a lovely ten- to fifteen-pound roast of tender, dark meat. Liberally sprinkle with all-purpose salt seasoning, then generously rub as much vegetable oil into the meat as it will hold.

A grill such as a Weber with air controllable vents on the underside as well as on the lid helps manage heat by regulating the air flow. A tin can suspended with wire from the grill's belly catches the dripping oil and prevents the roast from burning. Briquettes are ready when they begin to burn with a white ash. Add the roast to the grill, adjust ventilation to allow a steady flow, and cover. Grill for one to one and one-half hours, turning once. Like woodcock, it's ready when beefsteak is ready.

I cleaned the three woodcock I had shot that morning and added them to the marinating pot, turning the dark stew with a big ladle. We don't hang our birds or make a sauce from the trail but that's the next culinary step, I suppose. Every year we fashion a Henry the Eighth game dinner on Saturday, the last evening of camp, and the birds provide a pre-emptive strike before the main assault. It's the same marination we use for whole woodcock. We keep the meat covered in a cooler and turn it whenever someone thinks about it, usually every ten minutes or so.

At about four o'clock Ron and Dick came in, shaking the snow from their coats—for it had turned colder—and complaining about no birds. "They're under the junipers," I said, "trying to stay dry." But I knew they had no dog, a real handicap in this country of big timber.

A Fall of Woodcock

"Most of the guys are watching the game," Dick said. It's in the third quarter. Michigan's up 20 to 7."

That bit of news made me smile. Not because I care much about football or that my alma mater was winning. What made me smile was knowing that Norris and Jim were rabid Michigan State fans. A loss would only sharpen their appetites.

Ron savored the odor of roasting venison pouring from the Weber. He then unearthed a half-dozen heads of Romaine lettuce from another cooler and set about tearing the leaves into a huge stainless-steel bowl, the kind you see at smorgasbord restaurants like Country Buffet where two people are stuck in the door. He was building a Caesar salad, sans anchovies because he had forgotten to bring some. Two fistfuls of crushed garlic had been steeping all day in olive oil, "an enzymatic process," Ron explained, "that releases the true garlic taste."

In his mid-thirties, Ron is the youngest member of the camp and has just started a family at a time when the rest of us are girding up for grandchildren. Owner of a small public-relations company, Ron is a freelance writer, like most of us, but with an artistic flair. He designed our Bird Camp coat of arms, which I could just make out on his white sweatshirt, worn proudly like a food-stained apron. Arranged around the two-headed bird (grouse and woodcock, of course) is a dog print, a glass and bottle, and a crossed shotgun and fork. LMMGWC, (Lady Macbeth

Bird Camp

Memorial Grouse and Woodcock Camp, a name my friends decided upon when I lost that fine setter) is emblazoned above the circle. Grouse feathers hang to the sides. *Fiat Baccharalia*: Let the Excesses Begin! is printed across the bottom.

For the gamebird hors d'oeuvres I chopped Vidalia onions, carefully preserved all summer in my wife's pantyhose hanging in the basement. Meanwhile, Dick whipped up a batch of wild rice in a fat, black

A Fall of Woodcock

Dutch oven and began chopping a half-dozen apples to sweeten the creation. A retired schoolteacher in his early sixties, Dick is the oldest fellow in camp and has never missed a gathering of the flock. Retirees make the best bluegill fishermen, and Dick always brings fresh fillets for our opening-night salvo. He's more of a fisherman than a hunter, but I have noticed a steady progression toward vinyl-faced hunting pants and a sudden preference for double barrels. He is one of the fastest learners I know. I remember well the night he suggested that we bring our wives to camp.

Grumbles all around. Then stony silence.

"Maybe it's not such a good idea, after all," Dick said.

An eruption of cheers.

No one in his right mind would risk exposing a wife or girlfriend to Bird Camp, where testosterone vies with cholesterol for new personal highs. We eat what we will because we walk it all off (or some of it anyway) the next day. I've been in deer hunting camps where you eat like a market-bound hog, then fall asleep in your blind while a twelve-point strolls by. Or tumble out of your tree stand and bounce off the ground. The only exercise you get is climbing back up. But Gluttony quivers on Sin's scales when you repent with a vigorous workout, like a ten-mile jaunt through aspen slashings full of logging trash. Look at the Inuit subsistence hunter who has been known to clean up ten pounds of rich seal meat at one sitting. The next day he eats nothing while crossing miles of pack ice.

About five o'clock they showed up, lean and famished. Dave, who always reminds me of a Viking with his closely cropped red beard, had potted a couple of woodcock before joining the others for the game. "Take them home," I told him. "We've got plenty for snacks."

"Sure?" Dave said. "We don't want to go hungry. A guy never gets enough to eat around here."

An hour later after cocktails and debate over the game, we sat down to hors d'oeuvres. I had sautéed onions in butter in an iron skillet, then added mushrooms with chopped tarragon. After a couple minutes I splashed in a shot of Madiera along with the woodcock legs and boned breasts. With five minutes of simmering time to go, I stirred in a cup of heavy cream. When the cream turned clear, the woodcock were done.

Next came Ron's tub of salad, complete with grated Parmesan and homemade croutons pan-fried earlier in olive oil. Jerry suddenly disappeared, then returned cradling four bottles of Long Flat Red as though they were newborn babies. There is no more satisfying sound than a wet cork leaving a bottle of red wine like some tortured soul. Hemingway was wrong: There is no worry in opening bottles of booze. The time to fret is when the bottle is empty.

The venison roast was done just right; there would be no sandwiches tomorrow. Unknown to me,

A Fall of Woodcock

Dick had added a few handfuls of almond slivers to his rice medley, which made a great accompaniment. While the snow swirled around the tent flap (opened wide to counter body heat), we wiped clean our salad bowls with French bread torn from skinny loaves that went down one gauntlet and back up the other side.

Next, it was time for Betty Cake and Rita Pie, wrung from the generous hands of Norris's wife and Randy's girlfriend, respectively. Then on to cards and stories and a firelight reading of Corey Ford's "The Road to Tinkhamtown," arguably the best outdoor story ever written, especially when narrated aloud while cigar smoke mingles with woodsmoke and leaping sparks confuse themselves with stars.

Each year is different. Each is the same. I remember Ron's first grouse, a big red-phase male with black collar as royal as a medieval monarch's. Tom's excitement at finding and naming two new coverts—the Promised Land and the Triple Limit. Breaking my self-imposed three-woodcock limit to take five, in a row, over five consecutive points from a young setter named Fagin. Suddenly missing Holly, my old yellow Lab, and finding her curled atop my sleeping bag, body twitching from the exertion of hauling arthritic limbs over logs all day. Land Between Two Rivers. The Blow-down Cover. The Grade. The Big Burn.

I recall a young dog named Jackson Five, owned by an old hunter named Colonel Graham, who stayed in camp one morning, the northern tangles a bit daunting when you've spent sixty years gunning quail on golf-course-like southern plantations. "Jack" went along, and he had it all: courage, boldness, loyalty and obedience, wrapped up in a birdfinder's nose. It makes me nervous to hunt another man's dog, especially a priceless partner like Jack. So I put a bell on him and kept him in as close as he wanted to stay. Along a creek slope heavy with bracken fern still green, the bell went dead, and Randy, my hunting partner that day, and I lost Jack for a frantic ten minutes. By parting the individual fronds, we eventually found him, half-screwed into the ground, tight as a guitar string, a waft of bird scent running up his nose.

The exploding grouse startled us, and we missed our shots. I reached down to praise Jack, who had remained steady to flush and shot, and noticed that he had swapped ends. He was still on point.

"It's gone," I said. "Bird gone, Jack." But the setter, as tight as rivets to sheet metal, refused to budge. A well-aimed kick in the bracken in front of the dog dislodged the bird, a big woodcock. Randy and I never fired our guns. Later, when I told Colonel Graham the story, he was beside himself with pleasure.

It is experiences like this, and food not of this world that each of us lives for, our chance to grab mortality in a full nelson for a few days each October.

10

RESEARCHERS

"Ever since I first witnessed the male's spectacular spring sky-dance and hunted woodcock with a pointing dog, I have been intrigued by these fascinating birds." So says Dr. George (Andy) Ammann, who banded 1,580 woodcock from 1960 to 1995. For the first time in thirty-six years, he found no woodcock in the spring of 1996, but he was out there looking. At age 86, Ammann, a wildlife biologist long retired from the Michigan DNR, continues to hunt deer and wild turkeys with a recurve bow. He deplores the use of gadgetry and has killed three gobblers with his recurve. Reluctantly, Andy has given up shooting woodcock in fall with his 20-gauge double-barrelled Lefever because of a bad back.

But he still likes to go with others, carrying two ski poles for support, and his English setter, Patches, age nine, is as good as ever.

Son of O. H. Ammann, the famous Swiss engineer who built the Verrazano Narrows and George Washington bridges, Andy lived up in northern New Jersey where he explored neighborhood woods and fields. Building bridges was not in his future. Instead, the ten-year-old boy captured butterflies with a net and preserved them. He identified birds with the aid of a four-power opera glass and *Reed Bird Guide* and before long could distinguish the available species by their songs. Earning B.A. and M.A. degrees in zoology from the University of Iowa, Ammann did his Ph.D. work at the University of Michigan. His thesis topic was *The Life History of the Yellow-headed Blackbird*. The year was 1938.

Ammann began his career with the Michigan DNR, doing research in the Upper Peninsula, but was interrupted by World War II when he served as a captain in the U.S. Infantry. In 1945 Ammann went back to work for the DNR where he spent nearly thirty years researching birds and promoting sportsmen's causes, such as longer grouse and woodcock hunting seasons. His *The Prairie Grouse of Michigan*, published in 1957, is considered a classic on managing sharp-tailed grouse and prairie chickens.

"I became interested in woodcock because I felt it was a neglected species," he once told a magazine writer. Working with federal biologists, Ammann helped establish wing-collection programs and census routes in Michigan (there are 900 nationally), two important annual sources for information monitored yet today. In the spring of 1960 when his Brittany, Rusty, accidentally found and held a brood of woodcock, the idea of banding chicks through the use of pointing dogs took root. To date, the hundred or so licensed volunteer banders in Michigan, many of whom Ammann introduced and trained, have tagged more than 18,000 birds.

For several years after retiring he assisted other investigators, banding woodcock in early March in Alabama, then ventured north as the hatching season progressed. He found and marked broods in twelve states, before finishing the spring's work at Moosehorn National Wildlife Refuge in Maine.

Actually, Ammann was not the first researcher to band woodcock with pointing dogs, but he perfected a technique for capturing hens with long-handled nets. "Brooding hens sit very tight, especially when the chicks are small," he says. "If you approach carefully, you can capture some of them."

The key is to know when the hen is on eggs or actually brooding chicks. Disturbing an incubating hen can cause her to desert the nest, but hens with broods rarely do. Ammann's book, *A Guide to Capturing and Banding American Woodcock Using Pointing Dogs*, first published by the Ruffed Grouse Society in 1981 and revised in 1994, explains the fine points of this exciting, off-season hobby. In Lan-

A Fall of Woodcock

sing Michigan many woodcock hunters and banders belong to the Andy Ammann Chapter of the Ruffed Grouse Society.

On an early morning in late May of 1993, Andy Ammann and I roll north from his Haslett Michigan home in Andy's 1987 Volkswagen Vanagon (his seventh consecutive VW bus) with the sounds of Strauss emanating from a cassette tape beneath the dusty dashboard. Above strains of "The Blue Danube" Ammann talks about Katie and her daughter Dolly, two fine English setters he once owned that produced a long line of coveted birdfinders. Over nine seasons of spring hunting, Katie found more than 250 woodcock broods, allowing Ammann to band more than 800 hens and chicks. She once held a point for one hour and twenty-five minutes while Andy waited for the sun to come up so he could photograph the hen and her brood.

An hour's drive brings us to the Gratiot-Saginaw State Game Area where spring is bursting. Goslings in a family of Canada geese are already half the size of the parent birds. A cock pheasant crows from a nearby field, and marsh marigolds are in full bloom. I wonder if woodcock are done with nesting chores and what kind of luck, if any, we will have today. Ammann tells me that 90 percent of woodcock clutches hatch within a one-month-long period. In southern lower Michigan the hatching peak is usually late April but that sometimes broods are found into early June. I am hopeful.

Turning Patches loose, we walk through open areas while the handsome black eye-circled male scours the perimeter brush. Hens typically lay their four eggs within a couple hundred yards of the same openings where males peent and sky dance and mating occurs.

In late morning Patches bumps a brooding hen, which flies slowly away with tail tucked and feet dropped, an obvious effort to decoy us from her chicks. Using a keen-nosed, soft-footed dog that is absolutely staunch is critical to banding success. Of 109 banders who went afield during a recent spring in Michigan, 59 of them owned English setters (5 of the 59 also had other breeds). Brittanies accounted for thirty dogs; the others were German short-haired pointers (10), English pointers (4), German wire-haired pointers (3), Gordon setters (2), and a single Vizsla.

Patches seems to know there is a brood nearby, and he searches with careful diligence. A sudden hard point brings a gentle "Whoa" from Ammann, who pulls a pair of field binoculars from his shirt pocket. Finally, he spots a lone chick, which lies motionless no more than fifteen inches in front of the setter's beady stare. It takes me several minutes to find the bird, whose cryptic coloration blends perfectly with surrounding leaf litter. Andy carefully drops his net over the chick, removes the bird, and places it in a cloth mesh bag with zippered top.

A long, hard search turns up no others, an oddity of sorts because most broods contain three chicks and often four. Five chicks are uncommon and six are rarer still. When the phenomenon occurs, usually two broods of different ages have become mixed, perhaps because one of the hens has been killed by a predator. Unlike snipe broods, in which each parent takes two chicks to rear, woodcock males do not contribute to raising their offspring. Patches' find appears large enough to fly, a likely explanation for the disappearance of its siblings. Woodcock chicks can fly well at two weeks of age; at one month they resemble their parents in size and behavior.

Convinced there are no other chicks nearby, Andy removes the fledgling from the mesh bag. Carefully holding the chick in one hand, its head and long bill protruding from between his index and middle finger, Andy selects a USF&WS aluminum band from several on a wire. Using special long-nosed pliers, Ammann opens Band #1453-43752, places it on the chick's leg, and carefully closes it. Producing a small steel rule from his shirt pocket, he then measures the chick's bill while the bird remains completely docile. Bill length of a newly hatched woodcock is fourteen millimeters; each day the bill grows about two millimeters. Andy determines this chick is about fifteen days old.

Researchers

I have never shot a banded woodcock although several hunters I know have. If I ever do kill a banded bird, I hope it is not #1453-43752.

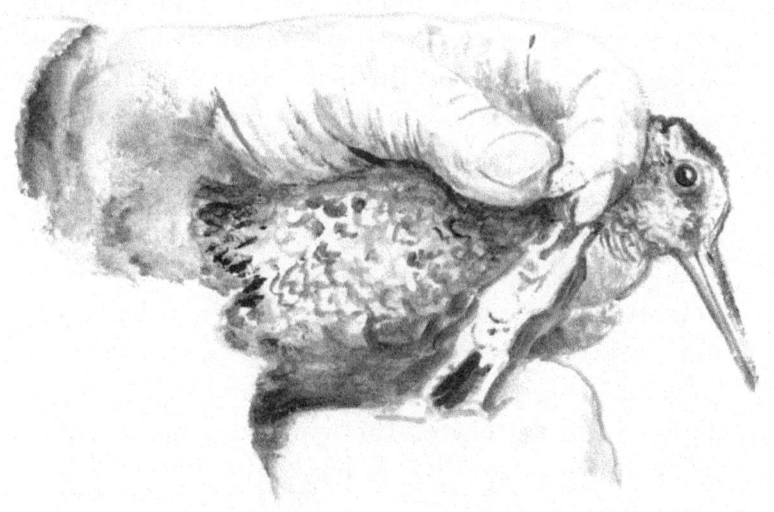

Ninety percent of all bands returned are from hunters, eager to know details about the bird they killed. Even so, they have reported only about 5 percent of the more than 70,000 woodcock banded in the U.S. and Canada since 1959. During a recent banding year in Michigan, a mere 34 of 824 birds tagged were killed by hunters in that same year—one from Quebec, three from Louisiana and the rest from Michigan. Although most banders are also hunters, the odds of killing a bird you tagged with your own hands are very rare, but it sometimes happens. In fact, it occurred to another friend of mine, Sheldon McBurney.

McBurney, who has banded 884 Michigan woodcock since 1978, found a hen on a nest on April 21, 1994. Marking the location with a piece of surveyor's tape, he returned on May 2 and discovered the hen near her nest. She didn't move, even when the net was lowered over her. Spotting her nest, which still contained eggs, McBurney realized he had screwed up. Gingerly, he removed the net without flushing the hen. Returning once more, on May 10, he learned the eggs had hatched successfully (unlike most birds, woodcock pip open the shell lengthwise—evidence of hatching and not nest predation), and he located the hen and her four chicks about fifty yards away. He banded all five birds and recorded the information in a notebook.

Eighteen months later, on October 28, 1995, McBurney, a retiree who hunts nearly every day in fall, shot this same hen, carrying Band #1063-13337, about a mile from the tagging location. Most volunteer researchers have a tender spot for woodcock; I'm sure that was a lump I saw in Sheldon's throat when he related this story to me.

Although the volunteers take great pride in the number of birds they tag, few boast of their success, in the same way that most hunters count flushes and don't mention kills unless pressed. The banders exercise extreme care in finding and handling hens and chicks. While attending a day-long spring seminar recently, I heard the audience emit a collective groan when the speaker announced that someone had stepped on a chick and killed it that morning. Accidents do happen.

Michigan DNR research biologist Andy Nuhfer is a passionate hunter and bander of woodcock. One warm afternoon in late May, his dog Radar locked on point a few feet from the edge of a ten-acre lake. Suddenly a brood of four flying chicks burst in all directions, and the hen started her broken-wing dance. One chick flew fifty yards out over the lake and landed, then began to swim parallel to shore. Nuhfer sank into the brush, hoping the chick would swim to shore. Closing to about twenty-five yards, the chick began to sink deeper into the water. Nuhfer tossed his camera and wallet to the ground and rushed to the rescue, fully clothed. He netted the chick and brought it safely to shore where it dried in the sun and suffered no ill effects.

The chick carried a leg tag, the same one that Nuhfer had attached nine days earlier.

Even though returns of bands to the USF&WS Bird Banding Laboratory are skimpy, the information is crucial to understanding the woodcock's habits and life needs. Do hens, for example, rear their broods in the nesting vicinity? Yes and no. Some chicks have been recaptured days later and only a few yards away.

However, a three-day-old chick banded by Sheldon McBurney was recaptured by another bander, Al Lowrie, sixteen days later at a location four miles east-southeast of the banding site. In another incident a two-chick brood was recaptured seven days later about two miles north. Why did these hens lead their chicks in a cross-country marathon of sorts? No one knows.

Most veteran researchers admit that far too little is known about woodcock. Sometimes observations simply lead to more questions. For example, do wild turkeys compete with woodcock for nesting sites? A volunteer named Ken Mohler flushed a hen woodcock off a nest of four eggs, then noticed a turkey egg one foot away. Six days later the turkey egg was still there, but all four woodcock eggs were broken and the chick embryos were dead. Did a turkey violate the woodcock nest?

What about deer? Does an overabundance of whitetails in some areas create habitat problems for woodcock? Especially when deer browse down young alder, aspen, and other desirable species, killing off the forest succession that naturally occurs in idled farm fields? Some researchers like Greg Sepik think so.

Hunters have long known that woodcock do not migrate *en masse* but rather individually although the urge to go often strikes birds by sex and age about the same time. Based upon my own experiences, I have always assumed that hens and juveniles tend to migrate before adult males, but a research study at Moosehorn suggests they may all go about the same time. Another study indicates, however, that young-of-the-year birds often travel farther south than their parents. Why? No one knows for sure.

Band recoveries are the core of such developing knowledge. They have also helped to prove that birds often drift to all compass points before heading south for good. Ammann, who once made *Ripley's Believe It or Not* by estimating that a tundra swan grew 20,000 feathers, is Editor Emeritus of the *Michigan Woodcock Banders' Newsletter*, now in its thirtieth year of publication. His curiosity never ceases. He recently determined, for example, that the heart of a hen woodcock is nearly identical in weight (about 2.3 grams on average) to the heart of a ruffed grouse. He continues to

do research on an earlier study by Michigan DNR biologist Doug Whitcomb which found that High Island, Michigan, woodcock increase fat deposits from 5 percent of their body weight in mid-September to 17 percent by late October.

Researchers distinguish between two types of band recoveries: *Direct* recoveries are those made before the birds' first winter; *indirect* recoveries occur after the woodcock have overwintered at least once. During a recent fall, four Michigan woodcock chicks banded the previous spring were killed at distances from 63 to 82 miles, either north or northeast of the places they were banded. Other long-range direct recoveries include a Michigan bird shot 600 miles east in Massachusetts. What was that woodcock doing there?

Andy Ammann's work in the South included banding an Alabama chick in March 1976 that was shot in Michigan the following October. A classic case of reverse migration! In March 1984 Ammann banded an Alabama hen with chicks, only to learn that a hunter killed the hen that fall in Michigan. Was she leading her brood north to produce a second set of offspring?

According to William Sheldon, European woodcock often raise two broods per year, but no one has ever proved that American woodcock nest more than once in the same season. However, one Michigan hen collected with large, flying chicks had enlarged ova, suggesting that she might have at least *attempted* another brood that season.

Yet another Alabama chick banded in the spring of 1984 was found dead in Quebec, more than one thousand miles north, in the spring of 1987. What caused that bird to wander so far from "home?" What was it doing in the intervening three years?

A woodcock tagged in Michigan journeyed to Quebec the next spring instead of staying home. An attempt to introduce woodcock to California failed although some of the birds traveled widely. One was killed in Michigan by Pete Petoskey, the former DNR Wildlife Division chief. Another was supposedly recovered in Kansas and a third in Alaska. Yet another anomaly: A Michigan-banded bird chose to stay in Texas into May and was eventually killed by a powerline. That bird was six years old. At least one other woodcock lived to the ripe old age of nine.

It is no secret that males often return to the same singing grounds year after year. The long-term record may be a Michigan bird, Band #1053-13670, that was captured in a mist net in Midland County during five consecutive springs. All these interesting facts, and more, are the result of volunteer banders and hunters who take time to remove the bands and mail them to the feds.

"Gordon Gullion was my hero," says Greg Sepik, a wildlife biologist at the Moosehorn National

A FALL OF WOODCOCK

Wildlife Refuge in Calais, Maine. "I thought, 'Gee, that would be neat if I could duplicate on woodcock what Gullion did on ruffed grouse.'" Sepik, one of the country's foremost woodcock researchers, is well on his way. Moosehorn is the only refuge of 425 in the national system dedicated to research and management of the American woodcock. In the twenty years that Sepik has been stationed here, he has proved that habitat can be manipulated to produce more woodcock.

Lots more woodcock. Use in some areas managed as feeding habitat has increased by 500 percent. In 1976, 72 singing males occupied the study area of about 7,000 acres. In 1995 there were 127 males, an all-time high and an increase of 43 percent overall. Success is even more dramatic if one counts from the all-time population lows of 45 and 44 birds respectively in 1981 and 1982. Given statewide population drops of up to 30 percent in some years, Moosehorn has been a steady producer of woodcock.

Habitat enhancement is the sole reason.

When Sepik first came to Calais, in southeastern Maine along the border of New Brunswick, Moosehorn's 22,000 acres were typical of forests in the Northeast. Old, mature stands of birch, maple, aspen, white pine, spruce, and balsam fir dominated in an environment where wildfire has long been suppressed, farms are abandoned, and forests are replanted with the sole purpose of producing pole-size timber.

Brittanies and Woodcock
by Jim Foote

Plate IV

Researchers

Sepik and graduate students from the University of Maine inventoried the management area for cover types and openings, soil textures and drainage patterns. Then they mapped out a program to cut long strips from seventy to one hundred feet wide to provide openings and feeding habitat on a rotating plan that would completely rejuvenate the forest every forty years. On the balmy October afternoon of my visit, Sepik proudly shows me the fruits of his labors. "This is one of our best cuts," he indicates with a sweep of his arm. "Woodcock really use this habitat when we provide it."

Were Sepik managing strictly for woodcock, he would not allow timber to grow more than twenty years before cutting it. But single-species management is out of vogue, especially on public land, and so he must consider the needs of other wildlife, both game and nongame.

A Fall of Woodcock

Young growth, particularly alder, produces the abundance of earthworms that woodcock demand, sometimes eating up to their own weight every twenty-four hours. Graduate students raising chicks in captivity found that each bird ate about $500 in earthworms. Intensive capture and banding activities have allowed Sepik to equip some birds with radio telemetry, which aids in recapture and in studies of feeding patterns, dispersal rates and habitat choices. He has learned, for example, that females, weighing only 200 grams when they arrive in spring at Moosehorn, need five weeks of feeding to get their weight up to the necessary 250 to 270 grams to lay eggs. When four feet of snow still shrouds the woods and fields at Moosehorn and woodcock return, Sepik expects some to starve to death.

Other observations and studies suggest that woodcock may have more enemies than those old culprits, the goshawk and the great-horned owl. In Michigan, volunteer banders watched a blue racer slither away from a nest after eating the entire clutch of eggs. A winter survival study in South Carolina and Georgia indicated that probable predators of radio-marked woodcock included bobcats, gray foxes, and barred owls.

Some of the findings that researchers compile are depressing. Consider, for example, two separate inventories in the province of Quebec, revealing that potential woodcock habitat made up only 3 and 4 percent respectively of the total areas studied. As evidenced by splashings, probe holes, and flushed birds, at least 80 percent of those habitats were used by woodcock.

The USF&WS estimates that the eight million acres of Northeast woods owned privately is larger than the combined holdings of federal and state governments *and* timber companies. If woodcock populations are going to reverse their downward trend, aggressive management practices must be initiated on lands both public and private. Making habitat improvements in the North, however, is not enough. The feds also estimate that up to 3,000 acres of habitat in the South is being lost *each day* to agriculture alone.

More grim news: Long-term statistics show a steady decline in woodcock populations. Singing-ground survey data from 1968 to 1996 indicate a long-term drop of 2.5 percent per year in the Eastern Region and 1.6 percent per year in the Central Region. Computed out over three decades, that adds up to major losses.

"The average at hatching is probably a little under four chicks per hen," John Bruggink, woodcock specialist with the USF&WS, told me. "Brood sizes seem constant from year to year, but somewhere between early brooding and the hunting season we're losing birds." Most experts agree that hunting is entirely compensatory, that the woodcock that go home to grace our tables would be lost to natural mortality anyway. This research project is one that Greg Sepik wants to undertake at Moosehorn, in much the same manner that Gordon Gullion studied hunter mortality on ruffed grouse at the Cloquet Forestry Center in Minnesota.

I do not believe we are overharvesting woodcock, but what do I know? I began to self-limit years ago when I found myself lying in bed after a successful hunting day and being unable to remember the details of the birds I flushed and each one I shot. The main reason that I kill fewer woodcock than the law allows—except for those rare times when a young dog is involved and there seems to be plenty of birds—is to play it safe.

11

Old Hands

He is a tall, lean man in the late autumn of his life. A modest, unassuming octogenarian with a firm handshake and steady gray eyes that hold, and penetrate. His large, gnarled hands have stroked the breast feathers on more grouse and woodcock than most of us will ever see. His eyes have seen more points, more flushes. His woodsman's legs have tramped more coverts, lean and not so lean, where live his favorite upland game birds, the royal ruffed grouse and the here-today, gone-tomorrow woodcock.

He is Horace G. "Tap" Tapply and he wrote the famous "Tap's Tips" column for *Field & Stream* for forty-three years and never missed a deadline. I grew up reading that rich, pithy column, month after month. Many of the outdoor skills I learned—reading animal sign as a schoolboy trapper, cleaning fish and game as a youngster, building a temporary shelter in my parents' suburban backyard—I gleaned from reading "Tap's Tips."

Tap Tapply always stood tall among my boyhood heroes. Heroes who knew how to shoot a running deer. Staunch an errant pointer. Tie a blood knot. Build a fire in the rain. Wise men who not only lived the experience but had the ability to write about it cleanly and clearly, without bragging, without embellishing.

Tight and bright was Tap's signature on anything he wrote. "I had five hundred words of space for "Sportsman's Notebook," he told me during a visit to his Wolfeboro, New Hampshire, home on a recent May afternoon. "Only forty to fifty words for each tip." His son, William G. Tapply, an accomplished author of mystery novels and an outdoor writer of his own stature, says his father wrote a total of 2,500 tips, every one of which fit the template of no less than forty words and no more than fifty.

I had always wanted to meet Tap Tapply, and during that long grouse-hunting trip to New England in December of 1989, I almost did. Over the telephone Tap arranged for my visit to his home, then in Alton, New Hampshire, on a Saturday one week before Christmas.

On Friday a blizzard socked New England.

Old Hands

"You're still welcome to come," he said next morning, the phone crackling from snow-weighted wires, "but be advised the drifts in front of my driveway are five feet tall. You could have a problem with your motorhome."

I went home. The years passed. Tap and Muriel, his wife of nearly sixty years, moved to the southeast end of Lake Winnipesaukee. The giants of our youth live forever only in our minds. Burton Spiller, who was born in 1886 and who hunted with Tapply for many years, has been gone since 1973. Gone too are Corey Ford, Ted Trueblood, Gorham Cross ("Grandpa Grouse"), and many of the others. Frank Woolner, author of *Timberdoodle*, died in the fall of 1994. But I am happy to report that George Bird Evans, who will be ninety by the time you read this, is still gunning his beloved Canaan Valley in West Virginia.

Tap was friends with many of these men and hunted with them and with Harold Blaisdell and Lee Wulff, and he fished with Ted Williams and Curt Gowdy, both of whom are still active sportsmen. Tap also once worked for William Harnden Foster, whose *New England Grouse Shooting* many consider to be the classic among classics.

Foster died in 1936. Tap Tapply is currently eighty-six. A spring wild turkey hunt to the Berkshire Mountains of southwestern Massachusetts puts me within four hours of Lake Winnipesaukee, and so I drive up to visit him.

A Fall of Woodcock

I could easily live in New Hampshire and feel right at home. It's like Michigan but with mountains. Real mountains, high enough that Clait Braun, a wildlife researcher and white-tailed ptarmigan expert from Colorado, offered to introduce the birds there in the early 1970s. The plan was scrapped because it was perceived as having little value to hunters. New Hampshire has a fascinating history, too. The thin topsoil north of The Notches grew plenty of White Mountains hardwoods but didn't support productive farms. After the Civil War, many of the farmers went west, and cheap land became available. Other waves of emigration occurred after both world wars, and the latest exodus continued well into the 1950s when dairy farmers were forced to convert to stainless-steel milking equipment or lock their barn in bankruptcy.

For fifty years abandoned farms provided Tap Tapply and his hunting pals a seemingly endless parade of grouse and woodcock coverts. Driving up from Massachusetts, I notice blooming daffodils, but the hardwood buds have yet to unfurl with new leaves. Spotting the ubiquitous stone walls, which nearly always denote former pastures—even when they disappear into now-mature hardwoods—I wonder if Tap ever hunted in this place or that spot.

He hunted in the best of times when access to land was easy and when farming and timber-growing practices waged war with each other, to the benefit of grouse and woodcock. "Brake for moose," the road sign says. "It could save your life. 211 collisions." I see the skid marks from a hammerjacking semi, perhaps as fresh as last night, and wonder if the driver was number 212. Moose inhabit mature woods. Mature woods don't grow many grouse and few, if any, woodcock.

Born in 1910, Tapply earned a business degree in 1932 from Northeastern University—where he picked up the "Tap" moniker—by working as a hotel porter, laboring in a mince-meat factory, and writing as a stringer for the *Boston Globe*. Afternoons found him covering Northeastern University sports, and when the game was over, he'd hop a streetcar for the *Globe* and turn in his story for which he earned twenty-five cents per column inch. "More likely than not," he observes with laid-back wit, "they'd run only the box score and I'd make the grand sum of fifty cents."

Shortly after graduation, he and a pal headed to California to make their fortunes. Tap went to work for the *Coronado Journal* and wrote a column about local events. These early newspaper experiences helped him hone his craft—writing with brevity and practicing the seamless art of invisible writing. While in California he came across a copy of *National Sportsman*, a Boston-based monthly edited by William Harnden Foster, who also edited the companion *Hunting & Fishing*.

Young Tap wrote a letter of introduction to Foster, telling him that when he returned home, he'd stop by and ask for a job. Every month or so he'd write again, reminding Foster of his plan. When Tap finally did return home, he made good on his promise.

Foster told him he had no work available. Undaunted, Tapply went back every couple of weeks. Finally, one of his visits coincided with the retirement of Edmund Ware Smith, managing editor. Foster hired Tap for $18 per week, not as an editor but as a gopher of sorts. It didn't take long to prove up. At age twenty-five, Tapply was appointed managing editor of *National Sportsman/Hunting & Fishing*, the new name for the combined magazines. The first article to carry his byline was "Rabbits Seem Kinda Small," a piece Foster made him rewrite thirteen times and which Tapply believes was finally published only to encourage him.

He made editor the following year when Foster died and in 1940 took over *Outdoors* magazine, which he headed until 1950 when new owners moved the periodical to Chicago. The year before, Tapply, friend Ollie Rodman, and a young editorial assistant named Hugh Grey put together an eight-page newsletter they called *Salt Water Sportsman*. Today that magazine is owned by Times-Mirror, which also owns *Outdoor Life* and *Field & Stream*.

Muriel met Tap in 1936 when she was working as a nurse trainee in a hospital and Tapply dropped by to visit a friend. Marriage followed two years later, and son Bill and his sister Martha were born in 1940 and 1945, respectively. When Tap lost his editing job in 1950, he didn't think he could earn enough money to support the family as a freelancer. So he went to work for a Boston advertising agency and retired in 1967. Meanwhile Hugh Grey, who had become editor of *Field & Stream*, hired Tap as a featured columnist.

The rest is history.

Tap retired his Winchester Model 21 about 15 years ago when an arthritic back and lame knee made walking difficult. One suspects, too, that after a half-century of climbing over countless stone walls, he may have tired a bit of killing the birds he loved so much. He speaks fondly of those days afield, though, and the light in his eyes grows brighter when he recounts the Brittanies Bing and Bucky, the setter Duke, and the other dogs.

Every weekend, rain or no rain, was set aside for hunting the Owl Cover, the Mankiller Cover, the Long Walk In Cover, the Tripwire Cover, and many others. Muriel, who often went along, remembers teaming up with frequent companion Burton Spiller. "I was his ears," she recalls, "because he was just about stone deaf."

Tap doesn't remember the first grouse or woodock he shot. In the tribute son Bill wrote to his father (*Sportsman's Legacy*, Lyons & Burford, 1993), he recalls what Tap said upon examining Bill's first-ever woodcock: "It's a woodcock," said Dad quietly. A lovely little bird....It's a shame to shoot them. Wish we could put them back, like trout."

Although Tap doesn't hunt anymore, his heart is in the right places. Spring evenings find him and Muriel watching the darkening sky in woods openings near home in hopes of catching a peenting male woodcock perform his aerial dance. I sent him a copy of my grouse book and videotape, and he said he enjoyed them.

"I'll tell you how much," he wrote in a letter, which contained not a single mistake, on yellow paper pecked out on his old Underwood typewriter, a relic he has used for more than fifty years. "So much I damn near cried thinking that I'm too old and too creaky in the knees to hunt—ever to hunt—grouse again. I almost wish you hadn't sent them. My idea of hell would be to read about grouse hunting and watch others hunt grouse—and woodcock, too, of course—while the devil taunted me: 'See what you're missing, Tap?'"

The Tapplys live in a modest home in a retirement neighborhood near Wolfeboro, one of New England's most popular resort villages. The town of two-thousand people, named for General James Wolfe of French & Indian War fame, swells to five times that size on summer weekends. I check into The Tuc Me Inn Bed & Breakfast, an old establishment that is reputedly haunted, then walk two blocks to The Wolfeboro Inn for dinner. The place is nearly empty, this being a blustery weekday evening a month ahead of the tourist crush.

    Small talk with a local, a regular bar patron:
"Where you from?"

"Michigan."

"What brings you all the way to Lake Winnipesaukee?"

"I came to interview a famous man who lives here. A man whose writing I've enjoyed most of my life."

"Yeah? Who's that?"

"His name is Tap Tapply. He wrote 'Tap's Tips' for *Field & Stream*."

"I know the guy! I mean I used to read him, too. He lives here? I've lived here all my life, and I didn't know that."

I don't draw him the obligatory map on a cocktail napkin. I think my publicity-shy friend would be pleased.

    Every bird hunter who has ever picked burdock from a partner's coat knows it will happen someday. But planning for the inevitable is no easier than predicting exactly when you will put the gun in the cabinet for the last time. The knees could go first. Or the heart. Sometimes your best friend quits, or dies.

    I know something about this subject because my own legs all but gave out last winter while climbing mile-high angular hills of live oak in southeastern

A Fall of Woodcock

Arizona in search of Mearns quail. The hills seemed higher, the legs more painful, than when I was last here ten years earlier. This time I cut what locals call a "Moses stick," a walking staff from the tall spire of dead wood that grows atop a species of agave called desert spoon. Reaming the rough stick through the sawtooth edges of the plant's bayonetlike spears smoothed it for splinter-free gripping.

When my legs grew so tired I could hardly lift them, the staff kept me from falling. But for awhile there I wondered if my bird-hunting career was over. It isn't, of course, but how does one really know for sure? Two older friends of mine from Silver City, New Mexico, are still going at it and they have twenty years on me. Dick, seventy-three, has hunted Gambel's and scaled quail for sixty years, mostly in the company of good Brittanies. "Three, maybe four years," Dick tells me. "Whenever Boots can't go anymore, "I'll hang it up, too."

"What about another dog?" I suggest.

"Nope. Boots is the last one."

Dick trades his gun for a camera on the second day of our hunt. So does his good friend, Mort, 74, who had half a lung shot away and lost several ribs during WW II. Mort came to the upland hunting game when he was sixty-five. "Dick corrupted me by training my dog," Mort says, pointing to Britt, his fine Brittany, who lies in the shade of the truck and pants with the desert heat as we talk. "Britt and Boots are the same age. I suspect we'll all quit together."

Old Hands

I think about my young dogs at home in their kennel and wonder how many others, yet unborn, will put up with me until I no longer want to go, or am unable to go. A close friend of mine, a man in his mid-seventies, put his thirteen-year-old setter to sleep a year ago last spring. For the first time since I have known him, my friend did not hunt last fall. He put himself to sleep this past summer.

"If you can't hunt behind your own dog, why hunt at all?" I remember him telling me.

It's a good point. The late Dr. Jim Hall of Traverse City, who was in his seventies when I met him twenty years ago, rarely missed a day in grouse and woodcock woods. The year before, he hunted eighty-nine days of the then ninety-day-long season.

"I took a day off to remarry," he admitted.

Some hunters stay with the sport into their eighties and beyond. "It's not a question of age," George Bird Evans, who began hunting grouse in 1925, told me in a recent telephone conversation. "It's simply a matter of having a little mileage." The late Art Currier of New York State last hunted birds when he was ninety-seven. Webb White of Boston, who has also passed on, was about the same age when poor health forced his retirement from field and woods.

These men don't go to kill birds although they say they kill those birds that offer an unusual opportunity or as an excuse to keep the dogs interested. They know they're full of it.

They go to see if the Blowdown Cover maple is as brilliantly red as they remember it.

They wonder if the wood ducks on their favorite trout stream have gone south for another year.

They want to smell again the sweet ripeness of fermented wild currant.

They hope to hear once more the pointer's tinkling bell, the *brrrrrrrr* of wings, and maybe to taste the coppery tang of gunpowder on autumn air.

Some quit the sport at a given hour of a given day. Others ease out over time. An artist friend of mine, now 71, has owned setters for many years. After losing a prize partner to old age, Jim did not hunt for two years, even though he had another good dog in the wings. Finally, last fall Jim picked up his gun again and was pleasantly surprised at how well the younger dog performed.

Count me among those who know that the best way to avoid the dreaded Nordic Track, for one season of the year anyway, is to follow a belled dog into a covert ripe for picking.

Legend has it that John C. Phillips, who wrote *A Sportsman's Scrapbook* and other fine books on the American shooting scene of the 1920s, died of a heart attack while approaching his dog on point. With the exception of slipping away in our sleep, is there a better way to exit this life?

A man I'll call Ben, with whom I used to hunt, died last fall on the opening day of Michigan's

Old Hands

small-game hunting season. Ben shot a limit of five woodcock, his favorite game bird, that morning. After lunch, the story goes, he went back in the woods with his son and grandson. Ben wandered off, supposedly to check a dog's dead bell. Ben shot a grouse and then tipped over from a heart attack. He was sixty-eight years old.

I always wondered if Ben would die in the woods. A high-energy man, demonstrative and easily excited, Ben swept through the coverts while hollering at his dogs and trying to manage our drive line of hunters. His goal was to flush every bird and to kill as many as possible. Ben hunted nearly every day of the sixty-day-long season, and he shot five woodcock almost every time out.

In truth, Ben was a generous man who hunted with many people, and for a long time my Octobers were never complete unless I stopped by to share a hunt with him. His sons and brothers bought him a case of shells each Christmas and sometimes a new pair of field pants so he could throw away the torn and frayed pair, less than a year old. I've never known anyone who pushed at bird hunting harder than Ben.

I quit dropping by when I began to realize that Ben's intense passion for hunting was, in reality, an unresolved anger. His rage must have gone back a long time.

During rest breaks he railed at the government and bitched out his ex-wife, the DNR, and anyone else who irritated him at the moment. The madder Ben grew, the redder his face became. The bulging veins in his forehead made me think of a check valve about to blow. Then, as suddenly as it began, the crisis seemed to pass and the tomato color drained from his cheeks. "Let's go hunting," he would laugh as though nothing had happened.

There may be a bit of Ben in each of us. Whenever I find myself getting a little too blood thirsty—something that can happen when woodcock coverts are so full your dog points a new bird while bringing back a dead one—I think about such things.

On the eve of his seventy-second year of bird hunting, George Bird Evans may have said it best during our telephone conversation: "The important thing is to hold a certain reverence for grouse and woodcock. We should never be the adversary."

If we are, we should try to figure out why.

Epilogue

Until you fully witness the male woodcock's sky dance, you will be deprived of one of the natural world's most spectacular events. Because I do not hear certain high-pitched sounds such as nasal peents and twittering wings, I had no idea what I was missing. Last spring in the Berkshire Hills of western Massachusetts, I got to experience the whole shebang, thanks to a borrowed Walker Game Ear.

No other bird in North America can match the woodcock's aerial ballet. Few equal his earnest efforts to attract a willing female.

Some friends and I were watching the western sky between sundown and dusk, waiting for the afterglow to change from orange to lemon. Then I

A Fall of Woodcock

heard it, the buzzlike peent of a male woodcock, like some noisome insect winding up for full assault. The peenting abruptly stopped, and I saw the woodcock, etched against the light, arc away over the trees. He spiraled back and forth, higher and higher, in an expanding gyre.

I lost him in my binoculars before he reached the apex some three hundred feet above the darkening earth. There was a pause of perhaps ten or fifteen seconds, then the chirplike sound the literature says is wind whistling through the outer wingfeathers of the falling bird. I saw him knife across the ribbon of light, in exactly the same place I had watched him rise a moment earlier. His serenade was as spectacular as it was sincere. Perhaps a female noticed. Maybe she rewarded his efforts by approaching the edge of the opening where he would find her and mate with her.

I certainly hoped so.

So many places. So little time. In spite of the many scattered locations where I have sought woodcock, there are many others I want to visit. One is the Canaan Valley in West Virginia where land managers planted autumn olive in a design that spells WOODCOCK when viewed from the air. Another is Cape May, New Jersey, which used to host thousands of migrant woodcock that paused to rest and feed before crossing Delaware Bay. Cape May still sporadically receives large numbers of birds, but find-

Epilogue

ing a place to hunt is next to impossible, and timing a visit is tricky.

A New Jersey friend, who has hunted the cape for years, promised to call when the flights were in. Over the telephone one evening in mid-November, he delivered the good news: fifty-seven woodcock flushed in only two hours that very afternoon. Then the bad news: A cold north wind, certain to strip bare the coverts, was already blowing.

A third spot on my wish list is the Delmarva Peninsula at Cape Charles, Virginia, where one of the managers at the Eastern Shore National Wildlife Refuge recently flushed more than four hundred woodcock in a quarter-mile…and then stopped counting. Many of these birds were apparently underweight, perhaps too tired to fly farther south, and they died in a subsequent ice storm.

And there are many other places I want to see—Cape Breton Island in Nova Scotia, Prince Edward Island, High Island in the middle of Lake Michigan, willow-covered islands of the Mississippi River in Tennessee, southern Indiana and its network of floodplain rivers like the Muscatatuck and White, the Atchafalaya River basin in Louisiana, the swamp country of southeastern Arkansas.

One never knows what experiences await on the open road. Driving back from a six-week-long hunting trip a few years ago, I was within a few hours of home when suddenly an aspen crashed to the ground along the forested highway. I swerved my truck to avoid hitting the tree. Shaken, I pulled over and got out to see what was going on. A beaver was apparently working overtime that morning.

Sometimes one incident leads to another, which is all part of that great adventure called travel. One time I stopped at the Michigan DNR district office of a friend of mine in the Upper Peninsula. A fisheries biologist, Bill, who at the time was in his forties, likes to hunt, too, but mostly deer. As a youngster hunting with his father, he had shot grouse and woodcock. I talked Bill into going again, with me. It was late afternoon—not enough time to race home and change—and so I loaned Bill a hunter-orange vest, a pair of boots, and my spare shotgun.

A few minutes out of town we chanced upon a birdy covert and flushed thirty-five woodcock and a dozen grouse in only two hours. Bill's smile looked like one of those exaggerated happy faces you see on schoolchildren's lunch pails. "God, that was the most fun I've had since I was a kid," he admitted.

We stopped for a beer at a local tavern where Bill knew everyone, then wandered on down obscure roads to a spot back in the woods where a friend of his was building a house. The carpentry crew were all Finlanders, each of whom Bill recognized and knew by name. No one was expecting us, but the instant we arrived the hammers ceased to pound and the saws went silent. Bottled beer suddenly materialized from personal coolers. Someone put a cassette tape in the boom box and we sang "The Second

Epilogue

Week of Deer Camp" along with Da Yoopers. I would pay plenty for a recording of the Finnish jokes that followed.

Sometime around midnight Bill and I landed at his home in Hancock. While Jeannie, Bill's wife, warmed chili on the stove, my friend and I cleaned woodcock and grouse. I left him a couple recipes and he gave me a jar of thimbleberry jam, which can be very hard to obtain some years in the U.P. Catching a couple hours of sleep, I left before dawn the next morning. That memorable day occurred several years ago, and now that I think about it, I realize I have not seen Bill since.

Woodcock will always intrigue. Another friend of mine told me she spotted more than a hundred woodcock along a muddy road one dark night in northern Michigan during the third week of June. "They were just sitting there, around the mud puddles," she said. "When I got closer with my flashlight, they flew off into the night. Weird."

A recent issue of *Condor* magazine reported that a team of researchers headed by David Steadman of the New York State Museum found woodcock remains in San Josecito Cave near Ejido San Josecito in Mexico, a few hundred miles south of the Texas border. Several wetland species, thought to be at least 10,000 years old and dating to the late Pleistocene Era, were also discovered. No wetlands and no suitable woodcock habitat currently exist in this area.

A Fall of Woodcock

For centuries woodcock have been attached to enigma. One of the oldest beliefs, which no one has successfully debunked, is whether hens are capable of flying away with chicks between their legs. Another is whether injured birds actually dress their wounds by applying a poultice of mud or other material. My Montreal friend, Michel Gelinas, has photographed woodcock anomalies for years. His collection includes malformations of legs and bills, healed wounds, and traces of albinism. Three photos show what appears to be unmistakable proof that woodcock pluck down and small feathers from their own bodies to make a dressing for leg wounds. I showed these pictures to woodcock expert, Dr. Andy Ammann, who shook his head in disbelief.

"I've never seen anything like this in my life," said the eighty-six-year-old ornithologist.

If you hunt woodcock in the secret places where they live, you will learn many things, some of which may change your thinking. But in the final analysis, do we want to know everything there is to know about this unusual little bird? I, for one, do not. Nor do I wish to know every detail about myself.

Some mysteries are best left unanswered.

About the author

Tom Huggler is a freelance writer and author of 15 books on hunting, fishing, camping, and conservation. His byline is familiar with bird hunters everywhere. The former president of the Outdoor Writers Association of America is also a successful videotape producer. He and his wife, Laura, live in rural mid-Michigan.

About the artist

Jim Foote is one of America's most celebrated wildlife artists. Trained as a wildlife biologist, he retired from the Michigan Department of Natural Resources to pursue a full-time career as a painter and carver. He and wife Joanne live in Marco Island, Florida, but continue to spend their Octobers in northern lower Michigan.

Woodcock Pair
by Jim Foote

Plate V